M000227467

Don't Feed the Squirrels

Reflections on how it was,

how it is, and

how it could (or should) be

D.B. Johnson

Illustrations by Lisa Phillips

Lorna,

Be proud of your contributions to
this great country. Appreciate in order
to enjoy.

Dave
12/22/14

Copyright © 2014 by D. B. Johnson

First Edition, November 2014

All rights reserved, including the right to reproduce or transmit this book or any portions thereof in any form whatsoever, without either the prior written permission of the author (except by a reviewer, who may quote brief passages). Requests for permission should be addressed to:

BEGIN YOUNG
PO BOX 1416
MARYSVILLE, WA 98270

Limit of Liability/Disclaimer of Warranty: While the author and publisher made every effort to be accurate in writing and printing this book, they make no representation or warranties with respect to the accuracy or completeness of the contents of this book and specifically disclaim any implied warranties of merchantability or fitness for a particular purpose. No warranty may be created or extended by any person or entity selling or promoting this book or by written sales materials. The advice and strategies contained herein may not be suitable for your situation. We advise you to consult with a professional if needed. Neither the publisher nor the author shall be liable for damages arising from a reader's use or misuse of the information herein.

Information or data presented in this book may have changed between when this work was written and when it is read.

Additional copies of *Don't Feed the Squirrels* can be ordered at
www.beginyoung.org.
Quantity discounts are available. Call our office for details, 360-659-1579.

All profits from sales of Don't Feed the Squirrels benefit
BEGIN YOUNG,
a non-profit organization assisting young people in maximizing their potential and capitalizing on opportunities available to them in the United States.

Learn more about BEGIN YOUNG at www.beginyoung.org

ISBN 978-0-9909064-0-7

Dedicated to my parents:

Jacquelyn Johnson
November 14, 1930 to September 10, 2004

Oscar Johnson
December 20, 1928 to March 10, 1999

Thanks for everything you DIDN'T do!

Acknowledgements

I'd like to acknowledge and give thanks to those of the past generations who have fought for, built, and preserved this great country, our unique and special rights as well as infinite opportunities. They should be proud of what they've handed over to us, now I just hope that one day we together can do the same.

I thank and am amazed at the talents and effort exhibited by Lisa Philips, the illustrator, for her creative ability to turn written words and messages into a more visual, uplifting and understandable form. Her typical comment was "I'll come up with something".

Thank you to my daughter Brandi for reading drafts and sharing valued perspective, insights and suggestions. To her and her brother Matt for all that they've taught me, and the fine example they both exert, making my wife and I proud and allowing me the ability and reason to write this book.

And a special heartfelt thank you to Marie English and the rest of my staff for the patience shown day after day as they continue to maintain regular business and without whose creative assistance I could not do without.

CONTENTS

INTRODUCTION

Don't be afraid to say or think, 'THE FIRST THING THAT MATTERS IS ME!' We've all heard the saying, "A happy wife, a happy life." How about, "All work and no play makes Jack a dull boy?" The fact is, there is nothing wrong with pleasing yourself, bettering yourself, or taking time for you. Say, for instance, you and your spouse take a weekend away from the kids or take some personal time alone to go to a museum, throw rocks on the beach, learn to sing or dance, or better yet, read a book cover to cover, and why not start with this one?

Read on and you might begin to open your eyes to just how important you are. You might see that by acting a little more selfishly and treating yourself to more, you may actually learn to be a much better spouse, parent, or citizen. When you look at your child, nephew, or maybe your closest friend and envision their life five or ten years from now, be assured that you and your influence will undoubtedly have helped shape their life for better or worse. You probably don't think that Kim Kardashian's escapades or any one of the 162 regular-season baseball games are, in any way, going to make a positive impact, but for many of us, these seem to take up a big share of our attention, time and conversation.

Time is a resource that we value so much and have so little of, yet we'll spend an exorbitant amount of this precious commodity doing repetitious things that will likely dull our minds and make absolutely no difference come the next day. Honestly, do we really care about the next episode of Dancing with the Stars, or for that matter, the entire Mariner season? There's spring training, pre-season games, and then 162 games to follow over a six-month period, not to mention that the same thing happened last season and the one before. Is this really the way we want to spend the next week or the last years of our life? An occasional television program or sporting event can be tremendously entertaining. But come on, six months and 162 games is more of an obsession than entertainment. Ask yourself, 'what else could I or would I be doing with those hundreds of hours?' The answer just may be what sets you apart and ahead of the millions of average Americans. Average, is that where we've set our limitations?

Today is the day. You will learn that we all have a few significant aspects in our lives that, if changed, would not only make us happier and much more prosperous, but would make us a much better example to the people we care about. The big changes, we all have them, but you'll be woken up to how it can be the smallest of changes in your life that can very quickly put a smile on your face, a pile of money in your wallet, or the largest gathering at your funeral. None of us can buy time, but we can certainly learn to acquire more of it.

Envy is an awful thing. You no longer have to look at others in envy and wonder why they seem to have it so easy, or why their children seem to be making all the right moves. You can make that mediocre marriage into a great one, have all the things you need, most of what you want, and never owe a dime. The knowledge you will gain in the following pages will allow you to better communicate with others who are knowledgeable, which may leave less time to spend with those old "going nowhere friends."

We each have to start with the understanding that, in order to truly enjoy anything, we first need to appreciate it, whether it is your car, spouse, children, or the country we live in. Believe me, I'm telling you the truth here, it is not that hard. As a home builder by trade, I'm used to thinking about a project in terms of steps. For a new home, it would go something like, Step 1: Draw the plans (8-hrs.); Step 2: Build the house (60 days); Step 3: Move in and enjoy (the rest of your life). Most of us go through our entire mediocre lives without a plan, when the plan could literally be drawn on a napkin. A small amount of effort today can pay enormous dividends for life. The kids will be gone before you know it. How do you want to spend those years, going to work or on a cruise? Would you like to be paying your car payment or buying a fine bottle of wine after enjoying a Broadway play? Do you want your children still on your couch or sending you pictures of your grandchildren playing?

But we can't just focus on getting you everything you've ever dreamed of, the wealth, health, successful productive children, and life of leisure without understanding that there are others around us. The fact that an overwhelming majority of people are so engulfed in Facebook, 200 television channels, and keeping up with the Joneses makes it that much easier for you and I to rise above and succeed. But we each need to be more aware and engaged in the state of our country and the world around us. There really is a huge disparity in the quality of life in this country, and while you and I may not fix the world, let's start with you. By becoming better prepared, healthier, wealthier, and especially wiser, we will be better able to improve the world around us.

We're at a point where half the nation is receiving while the other is contributing. Half can have no pride and the other half struggles just trying to not be angry. Both of them are feeling that they are not being treated fairly. Many have fought and died for this country, the least we can do is get off the couch, take a stand, and make a difference. Once you've achieved your wealth and personal success, which is the easiest of our tasks, then it's going to take us all to get our non-functional government working again, and the lazy back to being productive. Then and only then can we hold our heads high with the pride of the great nation handed to us by our parents and grandparents.

I'm just a regular working guy who one day opened his eyes to the amazing opportunities available here and nowhere else in the entire world. I realized that I (like many around me) was taking the wrong path; I focused and worked hard, all the while playing hard and enjoying the journey. I realized that life could be so much more, but first I had to change certain parts of my life. I invite you to take a few simple steps and re-align your life today and join me as we return this nation to its once greatness, and enjoy life along the way.

DON'T FEED THE SQUIRRELS

It was the 1980s, and my wife Erin and I were traveling across the North Cascade Highway leading from western to eastern Washington over what is said to be one of the most scenic mountain passes in America. I had made this trip maybe a hundred times before, traveling at nighttime with my brothers on the way to annual deer hunting trips in the fall and early each spring on the way to an annual trout fishing trip to meet up with family and friends. This fishing trip has evolved over generations from grandparents, parents and now Erin and I were making the trip with our two children. Erin and I had been working long hours in the weeks leading up to our much-anticipated four-day weekend. On Wednesday evening I rushed home from the job, emptied all the carpenter tools from my work truck and canopy , removed the ladders from the rack on top, and turned that truck which was our means of earning a living and feeding our family, into our version of a recreation vehicle – at least for the next four days.

The next morning loaded down with a tent, ice chest, and a few other pieces of basic camping equipment, including a large piece of Visqueen just in case of heavy rain, we were on our way. The kids, Brandi and Matt were in the back of the truck in the canopy, poking and prodding each other as they usually did, and as we started out, singing the song "We're on Vacation." About two and a half hours into the three-and-a-half-hour drive, we were hearing the usual "Are we there yet?" from the rear. What they really meant was, are we at the squirrels yet? At one of the steepest parts of the trip where the mountainous road switches back and forth with melting snowbanks, waterfalls and falling rocks on the road, there is a turnout where we never failed to stop.

That day, as in the past we all jumped out of the truck and ran to the rail overlooking the scenic view below. Brandi was always armed with bread, Hoody peanuts, potato chips or anything edible, with the intention of feeding the squirrels. The rocks below were full of squirrels, chipmunks, and other critters, just like we remembered. For Brandi, this was always one of the highlights of the trip and she anxiously waited for the journey home to repeat the ritual. She looked forward to it all year. Just like every other year, Erin said, **"Don't feed the squirrels,"** knowing it was going to happen regardless. Brandi, who was just a little mischievous, always tried to push the limit just a little. That day instead of throwing bread crumbs over the hill to the animals, she tried to entice them up onto the pavement until she could get one to eat out of her hand. Just then one of the squirrels took a little nip on her finger and she let out a girlish scream. Of course Erin had to quickly tell us all, "I told you so." This time there was another family there taking a break from their travels.

The mother grabbed her children, pointed at the sign that read **"DON'T FEED THE SQUIRRELS,"** and sneered at Erin and me as if we were the worst parents in the world for allowing our children to disobey the rules.

Later at camp, I explained to the kids, as I had plenty of times before, the reasons they shouldn't feed the squirrels, aside from the fact that half the bag of my favorite peanuts (Hoody's) were gone. I knew the reasons, yet I fully expected that in three days, we would find ourselves stopping and doing the same thing again. I explained that when humans feed the animals, it may cause the animals to become dependent on us, even to the point that they get lazy and don't have a reason to go out to hunt and gather; they might expect that the food would just show up. I explained how nature has worked for thousands of years; and even though we may think we are helping the animals by **giving them handouts,** it was really doing them harm. The only thing we were doing was making ourselves feel good, at the expense of the animals.

To this day, when my children travel that same stretch of road with their own children on the way to the same annual fishing trip, meeting up with Nana and Papa, they stop at that much-anticipated turnout.

Brandi and Matt are very responsible parents, so I don't know whether they would ignore the sign and allow my grandchildren to feed the squirrels... and I guess we will never know. You see, the squirrels are gone. My grandchildren will only hear stories of the way it used to be, much like other stories told by the elders over the years of how it used to be, the jobs that used to be, the industries that used to be, the stories of how this nation was built by the people who immigrated here.

The Department of Wildlife tries to manage fish and game populations in an effort to protect wildlife and ensure adequate numbers to support hunting and fishing activities for sportsmen. In the case of an unusually extreme winter, they may put out feed or hay for the animals to safeguard the survival of the herd, etc. Although this is messing with nature, I've got to think that offering this very short "safety net" is just plain good management. Throughout the rest of the year, leave the animals alone, and nature will take its course; no extended benefits, no permanent support, simply a helping hand at a time when they really need it. This is no different from any other government program; a little help when needed is good, endless involvement is disastrous.

FREE STUFF

After losing the presidential election to Barack Obama, Mitt Romney said, "It's hard to compete with free stuff." The signs are up everywhere, and we all know not to feed the animals, yet the signs are ignored.

Even though we can't count on parents to do the right thing and keep the children from feeding the animals, one would hope that we could count on our government leaders to protect the public from large-scale decimation of a species. I'm talking about the human race – specifically the hard-working American people. Many of our political leaders are spineless. How can they think it's a good thing to hand out indefinite unemployment benefits, unsustainable public pension benefits, or government subsidies? It's not only unpatriotic, it's treasonous for the government to be responsible for financially bankrupting this nation, running up debt to a point of no return, and creating generations of nonproductive, dependent people, simply to further their own political position. We're all guilty, and it's time we start fessing up and taking responsibility. You may be saying to yourselves, "I'm not guilty," but 'I'm saying to each one of you, wake up, think about it, and read on.

INCOME, WEALTH, OR EFFORT EQUALITY?

I voted for George W. Bush... twice. I'm not proud of it, but just like much of the rest of the nation, sometimes the voter has to choose between bad and worse. I chose to vote bad. I had been pleased with the intelligence, intentions, and leadership abilities of Daddy Bush, but two terms of Baby Bush and his cronies just about did us in. They set the Republican Party back decades and paved the way for Barack Obama to be elected. There is no doubt the American people were ready for change and that's exactly what we got. Look out people; this could finish off this nation, if we allow it.

More than any time in recent history, the last six years (the Obama years) have reversed the forward momentum of the previous hundred years. **The nation has been divided, in a way not seen since the Civil War.** The Civil War changed the nation in a few short years, creating fighting and hatred between neighbors, brothers, and all Americans. In subsequent decades the nation came together to defeat our invading enemies and greatly improve upon what our founding fathers set out for us; but during times of peace our nation still had numerous issues to work through. Through contentious political and sometimes physical battles, this nation continued to make amazing improvements in the area of civil rights, labor, and racial inclusiveness. Turning the corner at the beginning of this new century, though not yet perfect, the people of America regardless of race, gender, or sexual orientation had never before in American history, or for that matter in human history, been more accepting of each other, freer to exercise their rights, or freer from prejudice. We had a lot to be proud of. Then came not one, but two major financial setbacks: the bursting of the dot-com bubble, followed by the financial meltdown of 2007 and 2008.

Much like the years following the Great Depression, when people were hearing the promise of "a chicken in every pot," Barack Obama came along with words and phrases like "**haves and have-nots**," "**fair share**," "**fat cats**," and probably the most used and abused term "**middle class**."

SuperDuper
Size Me!

MIDDLE CLASS

The majority of the nation not only relates to, but believes they are part of the middle class. The problem is that the "**middle class**," as most people today think of it, **WAS NEVER REAL.** Over the last two to three decades, the people of this country have been enabled, and in fact, encouraged to create a life that was in no way sustainable. Nearly everyone ran up debt, from individual households, private companies, and more dangerously public pensions, governments from federal to state, county and city, and every utility and school district. **None of what we experienced was real.** This went on for so long that it was all people knew for most of their lives. If you ask almost anyone to describe the middle class, their view is probably skewed by this period of time, a period that in no way could continue to be sustained.

For "the working man," the expectation of just getting by has gotten much higher. Somewhere between the 1960s, when a comfortable family home consisted of 900-square-feet, one bathroom, a single or possibly a 2-car garage, to the 1980s and 90s, much larger homes, with nothing short of 2-1/2 baths, a family room, formal dining and living rooms, and of course at least a 3-car garage became the new normal. Anything short of that felt like the poor working man was taking it in the shorts.

To say that we as a nation have lived beyond our means would be an enormous understatement. In the last part of the 20th century, many households seemed to grow from modest comforts to two or more vehicles and a lot of toys, whether it was campers, boats, snowmobiles, etc. Just a fraction of people ever really paid for these things; it was all done using borrowed money. In the spring of 2000, as the stock market was tanking due to the dot-com bust, I recall George W. Bush coming on television and asking people to "go out and spend." This seemed to be the government's brilliant advice then, and it continues today with policies targeted towards getting money into the system with little thought about the long-term damage it may be doing.

HARDER TO GET BY

We hear it every day, how the poor working guy finds it harder and harder to get by. I remember when "getting by" didn't require a satellite dish on the side of the house with hundreds of channels available on demand. That's certainly not cheap. Boy, the poor working guy. For that matter, getting by a few decades ago went from listening to a radio, to black-and-white television with an antenna and a few local stations, to what most people have today, multiple flat screen TVs, which they now see as a necessity. In my case, until the 70s, our family had a telephone that came with what was referred to as a party line. This meant that when we picked up the phone to make a call, it would not be unusual to have one of five neighbors already using the one line shared by six households, in which case we would quietly hang up and try again later. If a friend or relative were to call from out of town or even twenty miles away, my dad would scream to the person on our end of the call that it was long distance, quickly state your business and end the call because it was quite expensive. After all, we were the middle class, the working man, and we watched our pennies. Our water came from a spring up on the hill, which basically consisted of a hand-dug hole with a plywood cover and a gravity fed line down to feed the family home. We didn't have a water bill or gas bill, and we couldn't have imagined the existence of a cable or internet provider. As we started to read about these new technologies, we in no way expected that regular middle-class people like us would one day view these as everyday essentials. My mom and dad both worked full-time jobs, which would explain both the need and the ability to support two vehicles in the family. Until I was in my teens, my family purchased only one new vehicle, and believe me, it had few if any frills. As a matter of fact, it didn't even have a radio, as that was an expensive option, and my parents, being working folks, would never have dreamt of purchasing an automobile before they could pay for it. That's right, up until the last few decades, people wouldn't ask "What will the payment be?" when considering the purchase of a car. My parents and my parents' friends never had car payments. They were middle-class working people. Dad's old truck had an AM radio that didn't require a payment to the satellite radio company to keep it functioning. People didn't have gym dues or personal trainers. The only auto repair bills were the major ones, as most people did their own oil changes instead of dropping by the mini-lube every 3,000 miles as we do today. People who complain about just getting by today can't or won't do basic chores. Too many people today cannot bake a loaf of bread, can fruits or vegetables, or even make a basic meal for their family without opening a box or jar already prepared for them. From spaghetti sauce to a pie crust, we no longer make meals; we simply open and heat them. One of the first sections we see when entering the supermarket is the deli.

As we stroll through the deli, we can pick out anything from already fried, fried chicken to potato salad or sushi. We'll pay $6.00 for a tiny container of macaroni salad which could have been created from about $.15 worth of ingredients. This is just getting by. One may say, "Well, not everyone is shopping and eating like that." I say, "Yes, actually I think they are." I've gone to numerous grocery stores and viewed others' shopping baskets. What's worse is that some of the worst shoppers and the ones with the highest priced junk food in their baskets are usually the young people who have free time, yet they can't even go to the effort of getting dressed and come to the store in their pajama bottoms and slippers.

The term "leftover" has been replaced by the terms "doggy bag" or "to-go box" since a majority of meals are eaten out instead of being prepared at home. Companies like Starbucks, along with other coffee shops or coffee stands are on every corner to serve up $4.00 cups to the same middle-income person who's complaining about just getting by. My mother, along with working a full-time job, prepared meals from scratch, literally starting with flour and raw vegetables, the basic ingredients. We were a family of six, with three boys and my younger sister, so Mom would cook as if she were feeding a platoon. At least twice a week we could plan on having "Desperation Dinner," which was a casserole consisting of every leftover thing from the past few days. Nothing went to waste, whether it was a piece of stew meat, a single green bean or kernel of corn. Then, when we were done with that leftover creation, there would be leftover leftovers. We were not alone, as everyone we knew did about the same. We were not poor, we were not rich. We were about as middle class as they came.

Back then, our family ate meals out about the same number of times per year as many now do per day. Maybe once a year the family would load up in the car and go to a drive-in movie. We would bring popcorn in a grocery bag from home. Mom would prepare hot dogs wrapped in foil, which Dad put on the engine of the car to keep warm. Today, it's not unusual for a family to go to a movie, purchase popcorn and soda and spend $50.00 to $60.00.

Growing up in the 1960s and 1970s, we never felt poor and certainly would not hear how the middle class was having it so hard. In fact, it was completely the opposite. Working families were seemingly doing far better than the previous generation. When my parents were starting out with a young family, a significant number of households included just one working member and a stay- at-home parent. Opportunities seemed unlimited when mothers could start working, sometimes part-time jobs and soon two full-time paychecks. Families could buy many of the things that the past generations would not have imagined, things like a washing machine and dryer, color television, and maybe even every few years a big vacation, something like a road trip to Disneyland. There were no complaints about hard times.

In the late 1970s, my wife and I were married. We were young, high school graduates who had never attended college. We both went right to work, from one job to another, always looking to better our position. We were two of the low-wage earners we hear and read about today. I'm certainly glad that we didn't have a president constantly telling us how bad we had it and how we weren't getting our fair share, because I may have believed that. No, instead we worked hard, long hours, saved a little, and strove to make ourselves worth more. We bettered our skills to a point to where we could earn better wages and then eventually became the employers, offering jobs to the next group of people that came along. Coming out of high school in the mid-70s, there were not a lot of jobs. Not unlike today, there were the people who whined and complained about the shortages of jobs. It seemed that if I wasn't too picky, and put enough effort forth, I was never out of work. I didn't have a choice, since there were no food coupons or welfare handouts for an able-bodied young man like me. I wasn't earning a lot, so if there had been handouts available, I suppose it would have been much easier just to sit and take what others had earned and complain about not getting my fair share. Society, the media, and especially the politicians were not poisoning our minds back then. They were not putting down the successful, they were actually promoting small businesses and people would actually look up to their employer instead of looking at him as some kind of criminal. In the coming decades, too easy access to credit and various other shortsighted policies started our nation down a path that most certainly got us off course. But never in all of the history of this great nation have we been brainwashed so quickly, to a point where there has been a wedge driven between what continues to be referred to as the "**Haves and the Have-Nots.**" The bigger problem with this wedge is the group of people who've been convinced that they are part of the "Have-Nots."

Anyone who may be thinking, believing, or worse yet, saying that it's getting more difficult for the middle class to get by should stop and ask themselves a few questions. For far too long, it has been too easy to buy things before we could afford them.

DON'T FEED THE SQUIRRELS

I'LL GLADLY PAY YOU TUESDAY

As a child in the 1960s, much like most children I suppose, I watched cartoons on one of the three network stations we received on our black-and-white television. One popular long running cartoon was Popeye.

Who can forget Popeye, with his spinach, the ever-present bully Bluto, along with the sweet (and somewhat homely) Olive Oil who seemed to be sought after by both Popeye and Bluto? Another character named Wimpy was presented as an irresponsible leach, or someone always asking something of someone. Wimpy's most common statement was, "**I'll gladly pay you Tuesday for a hamburger today.**" Wimpy seemed to spend his entire lifetime indebted for the hamburgers already consumed, never quite able to get caught up to the point to where he could just simply buy a hamburger.

Consequently, Wimpy, as one can imagine, was not a popular guy. In fact, people dreaded seeing him coming, as he was always looking for a handout. Cartoons such as this were broadcast day after day, year after year, always with the same focus on good morals, teaching us children, whether we knew it or not, good lessons. They depicted Bluto as a guy who cheated, didn't play fair and as a result, never got the girl. We would always root for Popeye, the underdog, knowing that before the end of the show, he would eat his spinach, get muscles and beat out the bad guy. Olive Oil was depicted as the no-frills wholesome girl that someone's mother might have picked out for a young man, not the short-skirted, made-up, big busted girl one might see televised today. But even back then, Wimpy, the guy who would always buy his hamburger before he could afford it, was seen as a deadbeat, a non-contributor.

Back then, the only real loan a person was expected to take out was to purchase a home. The typical person or family would save up 20% or more for a down payment, go down to the corner bank, and go into hock for the next thirty years. It was just assumed that you would occasionally pay double payments or additional dollars towards the principal and surely have that home paid for prior to retirement. Other than a home, loans were mostly limited to business purposes. It was almost unheard of to borrow money for any personal or consumer item.

Somewhere, in those coming years, car dealers began to experiment with offering monthly payments, sometimes enticing consumers with reduced interest rates, even no-down payment schemes to a point where one could sign their name and drive off the lot that same day with little or no money down. The dealer would work these extra costs, as well as the additional risk, into the price by inflating the price by thousands of dollars. They found if they did not act as the lender and simply acted as the broker for that loan, then as soon as that customer drove off the lot, even if they never made a single payment, it would be someone else's trouble. This is a practice that large banks and mortgage brokers later perfected, which led up to the financial disaster and housing bust of 2007/2008. People who, in the past, may have shopped for an automobile more out of need, looking for the most practical vehicle for the best price, stopped being concerned with the price as much as the monthly payment. They were no longer interested in the basic utility vehicle when right next to it was the loaded one with all the bells and whistles. After all, that loaded vehicle could be purchased for just a slightly higher monthly payment.

The dealers then began packaging those frills and gadgets into "option packages," where things such as an automatic transmission, AM/FM radio, power steering, power brakes, or electric windows were no longer available individually, but only as a package. It made it very easy for people to just go for the one with it all, to a point where today it's virtually impossible to go onto a lot and buy that basic model. All the extras have been worked into the price, along with the rebates, financing, etc., all for a low monthly payment. Some people may never question how the manufacturer can just give them a $3,000 or $4,000 rebate. You can bet that every $3,000 rebate has increased the retail price of that vehicle by much more than $3,000. And isn't it coincidental that the amount of that rebate seems to be just about the same amount as the required down payment? Now to sweeten the deal and sell even more of these price-inflated autos, dealers started lengthening the terms of the loans from 3-years, 4-years, and today to where you can finance a car for 6, or even 7-years; a new car, something we all know, greatly loses its value when driven off the lot. At the same time, manufacturers began competing with each other, offering longer and "bumper to bumper" warranties. In a very short time, people got out of the habit of ever having to work on their cars, or for that matter ever being responsible for the cost of a repair. As soon as an auto was nearing the end of its warranty, whether it was 3-years or 60,000 miles, a person could easily justify trading that car in for a new one. After all, by this time the loan terms were being offered for many more years, resulting in a monthly payment not much larger than the one they were then paying on their old car, the 3-year old one that no longer had the new car smell, and didn't have all the up-to-date frills offered on the latest model. The typical person would try to trade in that 3-year-old auto just to discover that they owed thousands of dollars more than it was worth. Well, the manufactures saw that coming, too. They pre-emptively started pricing new cars with the retail price padded by thousands of dollars, allowing them to give the customer a much higher trade-in than the old car was worth or than the person expected , another reason for the customer to justify the purchase. How many times have we heard someone say, "They gave me $12,000 for that old junker?" This is yet another reason that the prices on new vehicles are so inflated.

Thankfully, any even slightly intelligent person who enters a lot and is not planning on trading in their old car can purchase a new one for thousands of dollars less. Anyone in that situation who pays the sticker price is generally getting ripped off. The salesman will have all sorts of compelling stories or terms, such as $500 above invoice or, "you don't expect us to lose money do you?" The truth is that the dealer gets enough kickbacks directly from the manufacturer that, yes, they really can sell to you below the invoice they show you and still do very well. But, just like most consumer financing schemes of the last couple of decades, this couldn't last forever. After the first upside down trade in, a person may experience another even more upside down trade-in, and then the scheme no longer works. The person is stuck with a worn out vehicle that they can neither trade in nor sell due to the fact that they owe twice what their car is worth.

So, given this unsustainable system, you would have thought that the auto industry would have hit a wall; business is over, everyone is upside down on their car, and the scheme no longer works. Well, along came home equity loans. The government put such an emphasis on promoting home ownership that America went from 60-62% homeownership to nearly 69% homeownership. Though it was called homeownership, many never really did own their home. You see, a similar farce was happening in the real estate industry to that in the auto industry. A person was not only able to purchase a home, regardless of their financial ability to repay, their down payment, or in some cases without proof of employment, prices were being driven up by a ridiculously unsustainable financial system, and buyers were able to suck (perceived) equity out of their home to pay off that car or other consumer loan and start the process all over again. One could purchase a home with little or no down payment, inflate the purchase price of that home to not only include most if not all of the closing costs, but in some cases even purchase the much-needed new refrigerator, window blinds, and even pay off their credit cards and other consumer debts that would have prevented them from qualifying for the loan in the first place.

During the bulk of these years, the nation was in a declining interest rate environment, spurred by our government in an effort to get people to continue their spending. Just a very short time after a person had purchased their home they would get an appraisal that said the home had increased in value by tens of thousands of dollars. This not only made the person feel wealthy, spurring them to be more in a spending mood, but with falling interest rates, they had a reason to justify refinancing.

Now, as things were going on like this, very few people actually refinanced their house at a lower interest rate and lowered their payment or even shortened the term. Instead, they found that for about the same monthly payment they were currently paying, they could refinance their home and at the same time take out enough cash to pay off some of their other payments, many of which were at higher rates, thereby lowering their monthly out-of-pocket costs. They went home that evening and cracked open a bottle of champagne, thinking that they were a financial genius. The champagne, of course, was charged on the same or new card, just starting the process all over again.

The thing that they may not have realized, or possibly didn't want to admit to themselves, is that they just tacked on the debt of that upside down car loan, or the latte they put on the credit card the day before, to the tail end of their home loan. Now, they could conceivably be paying interest for the next 30-years and possibly never payoff the cost of the latte or the sweater, new shoes or the blender purchased yesterday or for that matter sometimes years earlier.

This refinancing or the second or third mortgages were not simply for the purchase of the home but actually were thirty year loans to fix or cover up all the bad deeds these people had been doing for the past few years. This would give them a clean slate and enable them to go out and get a purse full of new credit cards, two new cars, again, and dig a deeper hole. The whole time the news reports would tout this strong economy and it seemed like it would last forever. Lots of consumer purchases meant that public company stocks would go up, which in turn would make people feel wealthy again and spur more spending. It was only a matter of time until it would all come to an end, or would it?

With the exception of the very, very poor, everyone seemed to be at the trough. These were mostly middle income people, or at least people who considered themselves to be middle income. They were living the life! This was a life that was never real, but yet it felt like it was in their grasp; these people, after so long, thought that **this is how middle-income Americans deserved to live**, and they have been told that they are going backwards, or losing ground.

During that period of time, I can remember my son talking to me about purchasing a John Deere riding lawn mower from Home Depot. He had recently left college, was working long hours and was building a new house on an acre-sized lot. The small push mower just wasn't going to cut it. Since the price of the mower was a couple thousand dollars, he took the purchase pretty seriously. He told me "Dad, I could have financed the mower for thirty years if I'd wanted." Finding that hard to believe, I asked him about it. He said that they had offered to sell him the mower and gave him incentives if he would open a new Home Depot credit card, make the purchase on the new card, and then make easy monthly payments. At 23 years old, he knew how this worked. He said, "Dad, I only have to make the monthly payments. I technically will never have to pay off the principal. Furthermore, once I have the card, I can forever going forward, make additional purchases, and continue to just make the minimum monthly payment. The problem is that, thirty years from now, I will never know if I'm paying for my mower, or the next bag of grass seed I just bought." He was not even tempted, and he paid cash for his mower. He did, however, seem genuinely concerned that this system existed where people could finance a lawnmower for thirty years. I was very proud of him. Because of that way of thinking, a few short years later, he is now in far better financial condition than most, if not all of the people with those cards in their wallet or purse. As for the mower, oh, that gave out a long time ago. It wasn't worth fixing, but thankfully not having those monthly payments and interest to pay, he had saved enough money over the years so he can hopefully forever and always purchase a new mower from time to time, and never have a payment. Apparently all he had to do was watch and listen to gain the insight that is so often missed or ignored by others, this being just one of the many small mistakes in judgment people make every day that negatively affects their future lifestyle and prohibits them from ever experiencing financial freedom that, much like any other freedom, never comes without some type of sacrifice.

How many people have made a purchase and put it on a credit when they had an equal amount of money in a bank, earning very low if no interest? People every day have savings accounts with XYZ Bank earning almost nothing, but will pay a high rate of interest on an auto loan or credit card, essentially borrowing their own money back at a much higher rate. It doesn't matter if it's the same name on the bank or institution; it's the whole financial system. Anyone who has ever done that or who is presently doing that should be ashamed of themselves. At the very least, we shouldn't hear from them anything like, "Poor me, we're having a tough time just getting by."

Then along came President Obama and an administration who found it politically popular to feel sorry or show compassion for all the people who had acted so irresponsibly. After all, this group was comprised of a large portion of the nation, in virtually all age and income categories.

PREDATORY LENDING OR
PREDATORY BORROWING?

We've heard so much now from President Obama about these poor homeowners who were taken advantage of. These poor people who were handed gobs of money, who then extracted tens of thousands, sometimes hundreds of thousands of dollars out of the so-called equity in their home, to buy toys, pay off credit cards, take exotic vacations, or virtually anything else they chose to waste it on.

For some time, people were looking at a home purchase not as a place to live or for security for their family, but as an investment, more like a gamble that the value would increase and they could make that big score. And much like any other gamble, whether it's a bet on a race horse or the purchase of stock in a public company, you would think that the gambler should be willing to suffer the loss if he is there to prosper from the win. Just like investors who've purchased stock in Apple or Google, some bought at $50 per share and ran it up to $500. Some sold somewhere along the way and profited from their risk, some will continue to hold the share purchased on the gamble that it will increase even more. Others may wait on the sidelines, watching as others take the risk and over time are making money, until finally one day, they just can't stand to see someone else doing well while they are missing out, so they may buy in at, say, $400 or $500 per share, obviously putting their money at more risk than the person who purchased at the lower price. Millions of people did exactly the same thing in the home purchasing scheme. There was and never has been any guarantee that home prices would go up forever, but people, not wanting to be left out, would jump in out of greed. Rarely did people purchase just the minimum that was required for a roof over their head. After all, if they were to gamble twice as much and buy a house twice as big, they stood to get rich quicker, and besides, many were just expecting that they would turn that home over in a few short years, make tons of money and do it all over again, maybe with two or three homes. The reality is that many did just that, but even more failed.

My Brother has a term that I get a kick out of, and that's "**Hoggy Hog.**" He'll use this term when describing the lazy woman ahead of him at the store, three or four kids in tow, ordering up three large pizzas loaded with all the toppings, holding up the line while he's there trying to buy the basic one topping pizza that's on special that day. Inevitably, she is purchasing with her EBT card, the equivalent of food stamps, as he's trying to pay cash. He's paying with cash earned after a long hard day of work as well as a long commute. Assuming that this Hoggy Hog probably doesn't work and has all the time in the world, he's wondering not only why she should be able to buy these huge pizzas with our tax dollars, but shouldn't she at least have to step to the end of the line and allow the people who are paying for her lazy lifestyle to get their food, get home, and get a little time to sleep so they can get up the next morning and go earn the money that this Hoggy Hog is spending?

Hoggy Hog is what I think of every time I see someone receiving free stuff when they are perfectly capable of earning their own. The term Hoggy Hog could also be used when thinking of the tons of people who "pigged out" on the easy money during the housing boom, just to be there with their hand out for bail-outs when the president decided that, 'Oh, these poor people are losing their homes, and we need to ease their pain.' If a person had risked their own money and purchased a share of stock for $500, and the value had gone down to $400, I don't think most people would expect the government to borrow money and ease their pain by covering their loss. After all, they were certainly willing to accept any gain that may have come their way. Furthermore, every penny that the government would cover would be borrowed, since **our government has no money**.

In terms of the Hoggy Hog mentality impacting the real estate industry, many people purchased their home, very quickly refinanced, sometimes with one, two or three loans, and many times they attached a home equity line of credit option on the loan. This allowed them to essentially **use their home as a piggy bank** to extract money anytime, for anything. Our current president, never having any prior experience in anything other than as a "community organizer," knows very little about anything, with the exception of how to rile up the population of this once-great nation. He spoke of these "home loans" as if the dollars they owed had actually been used to purchase these people's home. In many, if not most cases, this was simply not the case.

Our president also found that it was popular to show compassion for the poor people who had run up tens and sometimes hundreds of thousands of dollars in student loans. Again, he would speak of these loans as if they were used for tuition and books. In most cases, student loans were just that, loans made to students. If a loan was made where the dollars borrowed were released directly to a university and university book store, they could be referred to as college loans, but instead the proceeds in many cases went to pizza and beer or simply money to support a student while being enrolled in college. I'm not sure when the phrase "**working your way through college**" went out of style, but there was a time when, unless a person came from an extremely wealthy family, it was just expected that they may work one or more jobs while attending school, even though it may take them a little longer to get that sought-after degree. I know both my son and daughter worked on weekends as well as all through summer and every other vacation to earn all of their spending money while in college. Now, since the president finds it to be politically popular, he wants to forgive, or basically pay-off these people's **pizza/beer loans**, again by having the government go out and borrow more money.

It's not a coincidence that the term "spring break" came to be thought of as college kids going crazy on some exotic beach someplace their parents couldn't afford to visit, **about the same time that student loans became so easy to obtain.**

Every time the government pays a single penny or billions of dollars, they are using borrowed money. The government, however, doesn't have to go out and apply for and "take out" a loan for some politically popular action, since they continue to sell debt (borrow money) several times a week, almost on a daily basis. They do, however, have to set a budget, and when the budget surpasses the tax money extracted from hard working Americans, (at least the 50% that actually pay taxes) as it always does, they need congressional approval to raise the debt limit. Between our current administration, as well as our entire ever-growing, liberal-leaning government, it has gotten to a shameful point where we seem to always come to literally shutting down the federal government, or nearly shutting it down, each time it comes up. The conservative government leaders (mostly Republican) being the minority, get ridiculed if they even dare to speak of limiting or reducing any handout programs. The reason for the outcry is simply that we have reached a time when there are as many or more people receiving than contributing. It is so politically unpopular to speak against limiting free housing, free food stamps, or trying to limit unemployment insurance compensation to some kind of reasonable length of time. Democrats have gotten people so dependent on these freebies and hundreds of other temporary hand-outs **(free stuff that should be referred to by no other name than welfare)**, that anyone who even talks about limiting handouts risks losing an election and becoming unemployed themselves. Those with the guts to stand up for what they know is right should be applauded and supported. The rest, who are too spineless and are only looking after themselves, should not only be ashamed, but should be run out of office. But, it's really hard to do that when more than half the general population of the country is on the take.

However, let's not go so far as to say that everyone who receives any sort of government assistance or payment is a Hoggy Hog. There are good reasons for many of the programs and certainly a need for government and government programs, it's just that they have gotten so far out of control that it has become shameful.

The majority of American people today just don't put enough thought into what's going on in their own nation. They really are too busy with Facebook, reality shows, and "how does this affect me?" to stop and think about right and wrong.

Every penny spent by our government today needs to be borrowed today. We have not paid for yesterday's expenditures, last week's spending, or for that matter, the last decade's frivolous spending. We borrow money on a daily basis just to pay the interest on the money borrowed yesterday and in past years.

Every day we continue to spend without a plan to fix our financial problems. It seems just too obvious that the first step to at least slowing the problem would be to not spend. How about spending less? How about spending only on the essentials? Seriously, at the very least, what we need is just one good leader, someone who can reverse the direction, muster up support from both political parties, and inject a little common sense into the operation. Sadly though, it seems unlikely that this will happen any time soon when the majority of people of this country, **the majority of voters are receiving "stuff" and are unlikely to elect someone who may threaten to take away the feeding trough.**

FAIR SHARE

President Obama has popularized the term "fair share" to a point where over half the nation, not just the Hoggy Hogs, is convinced that they are not getting their fair share, and most, almost all of the nation's people are convinced that the rich don't pay their fair share. If a particular middle-class person believes that the rich don't pay their fair share, then they must actually be under the illusion that they are paying more than their fair share.

My wife and I drive a Dodge pick-up and a Chevrolet SUV, live in a nice but not extravagant house, and just recently purchased a vacation home. We've both worked jobs from the time we were 12 years old, sometimes doing work that others would never do. My wife has cleaned other people's homes, worked clerical and manufacturing jobs, and advanced to managing the administration of our business ventures, and she still cleans our home. I've done ugly, nasty, dirty work. At one time, I quit my steady $5.50 per hour job to take a job that paid $3.50 per hour in an effort to get into an entry level job where I could learn a trade and better myself. It didn't involve a government paid training program or subsidized living expenses. I, like many other hard-working Americans, started from the bottom and paid attention to my surroundings, learned the trades, became more valuable, to a point where I could demand higher compensation. I went to work in construction, building houses. There was no government guarantee that would assure everyone was paid the same. We were basically paid according to how hard we worked, how much we got done, and the quality of the work completed. I was young, worked and learned fast, and quite often would be paid much more than guys decades older and with many more years of experience. I was just out of high school in the early 70s, and work was scarce, or so I heard, even though both my wife and I were working when many weren't.

Through the years we've started several business enterprises, not all of which were successful. Long story short, we spent from 1983 until today building and selling new homes, sometimes renting homes when necessary, to a point where we completed more than 4,000 homes over a span of thirty years. During this time, we were able to successfully raise a family without government daycare or other assistance by juggling our schedules and doing what hard working Americans have done for hundreds of years. Sometimes I would come home tired and muddy from work, as Erin handed off the parenting duties and headed off to work late into the night.

We have succeeded where many have failed, and it would be nice if I could chalk it all up to working harder, or being smarter. Over the years we have employed literally thousands of people, sometimes on our own payroll or many times indirectly through subcontractors. We operated our business as a small business in a big way, almost exclusively employing small contractors. Many of the subs were two-man operations, guys starting out like us; some were small businesses with five to twenty-five employees. We've had hundreds of direct employees over the years, some who've left for various reasons, and some who've returned, others who have retired or passed away. We ran our business to make a profit and stay in business, which could only be done by paying fair compensation to retain the best people, but not overpaying to a point of going out of business. I think most reasonable people would agree that this is in the best interest of both the manager-owner as well as assuring the ongoing employment of the work force. Any positions in our operations have always far exceeded any federal or state minimum wage requirement. Since, like most all single family construction operations, we were not unionized, and until recently no one, government or otherwise, told us that we had to pay each person the same, regardless of their capabilities or effort. There has always been a great variation in the pay scale between employees, sometimes even when performing the same tasks. As the owner of a competitive company, I can honestly say that no one was ever over paid, at least not for any length of time. We had the pleasure of employing some of the absolute best, most skilled people over the years, some of whom I could have never paid enough to compensate for what they brought to the table. Some may have come and worked for a short time, while others have worked with us for 10, 15, and 20 years.

We also owe a great debt to many who were not with us to the end, some who were laid off in the great housing downturn of 2008, and even some that may have been fired over the years; but without a doubt, our employees, our subcontractors and our suppliers, have allowed us to succeed.

I think if you were to ask any long-term employer or business person, they would agree that it is the people aspect of the business that we both love and hate the most. Whether it be the customers, employees, local government personnel, subcontractors or suppliers, real estate agents, or any of the hundreds of others we have to or get to deal with, the people have been what's made it both worthwhile, and at other times extremely trying.

After a lifetime of hard work and always reinvesting everything we made back into the business instead of frivolous spending, we have reached a point in our mid-fifties where we're financially comfortable. Up until recent years, we have been proud to be the business owner, employer, and generator of jobs.

Yet, since Barack Obama has come onto the scene it's actually gotten scary. It's become very unpopular to be "the man," "the boss," though we're still small business owners. The difference is that all business owners seem to get grouped into the same "Wall Street" or "CEO" stereotype (not that there is anything wrong with being CEO) to be frowned upon, even hated. Not only business owners but it seems that anyone who works hard, betters themselves to a point where they gain some degree of wealth is to be shunned.

I've worked and paid taxes to the Federal Government under the leadership of presidents from Nixon, Carter, Reagan, Bush, Clinton, and then yet another Bush, (the second of which I was not too happy with), and I've been happy to contribute more than my fair share, even knowing that the tax dollars were rarely being spent as wisely as we would all expect. Working under each and every one of these accomplished leaders,

I always felt as if I was being treated with the respect and dignity I deserved. Being a small business owner, an employer and taxpayer, I was encouraged and, to some degree, honored. I was actually proud to be an American businessman. Now, under Barack Obama, we actually feel like we've been humiliated and demeaned to a point where we're actually scowled at by a large portion of the population. At my age, I can imagine that I could continue to operate my business for decades to come, but I just can't see myself working for this president, so I QUIT! I just can't continue to work for this guy any more than an employee would work for an employer for whom they have no respect, or who they view as having questionable morals, poor intentions, or inadequate intelligence. My ongoing concern is that our nation has been damaged or desecrated to a point that the majority of the people now think only, 'how does it affect me?' They will probably elect another president who will promise them free stuff. Mitt Romney had it right when he said, after losing to Obama, "It's hard to compete with free stuff."

So, under the previous leadership of this nation, people like us were able to work hard, save, and invest our after-tax dollars, provide thousands of jobs, generate millions of dollars in taxes of all sorts, from federal, to state, city, along with sales tax, property tax, and numerous other fortunes contributed to society. We were able to do all this while also prospering ourselves, along with countless people who supported us while being supported. We did all this while watching our contributions work towards the continuation of our nation's prosperity and growth that so many Americans before us successfully fought and worked for.

This great nation, along with the free enterprise system that so many have preserved and improved upon for hundreds of years have allowed my family to financially prosper to a point that may be only obtainable in some people's dreams, much like the dreams of the people who have been coming to America since and before its inception.

We've become one of a small fraction of people who risked everything over and over and were lucky enough to make it. Though I feel no different than I have for the last thirty years, with the exception that I can drive a newer model pick-up truck, we are now in that narrow category of "the rich," maybe what is today suddenly referred to as the one-percent, **as if it is something we should be ashamed of**. Up until recent years, I would have been proud of our achievements and would have been able to hold my head high. Today, I feel the need to hide out of fear and banishment.

What makes things even worse is turning on the television and hearing, not once, not even occasionally, but constantly hearing our president telling the American people that the rich aren't paying their share. It has quickly spread to a point where I often find myself in social situations, sometimes even with close friends, where someone is repeating in ignorance that "the rich don't pay taxes" or "they should pay their fair share." It sickens me to hear that kind of ignorance being spoken by people who, I'm guessing, mean no harm, but have simply been misled and are repeating the words they've been fed. Many of these same outspoken people actually think of themselves as burdened tax payers, when they pay nowhere near their own fair share, if any taxes.

Though I'm sure there may be some large corporations, and maybe a handful of Wall Street bankers that pay less than we all may think is right, there are thousands of regular people like us that have, for years, paid more federal income tax each quarter (that's every three months) than many complaining people actually earn in an entire lifetime. Should I be ashamed of that? I don't think so. After all, who else will create the jobs? If hard working Americans are not allowed to make and keep something more than the guy who chooses to drink up his paycheck every Friday night at the local bar, what incentive will there be to continue the entrepreneurism and innovation that this country has known for hundreds of years?

The fact remains that very few pay almost all of the federal taxes. For the most part, it is not the regular working guy who pays most of the taxes. Nearly half the people in the nation don't pay a penny into the federal tax system, but they continue to live a life in this country that people in other parts of the world would consider equal to the life of a king or queen. And now they are complaining after continually being told that they aren't getting their fair share. I say that, for the majority of these people, their fair share is exactly what they contribute to society: zero. **Then there is a large block of contributing, working tax payers who pay nowhere near what they should. This is not a few people I'm talking about, but most people.** The bulk of people receive much more value and service from this nation then they pay for. Though it's been a great deal for these people (most of the nation), it is not sustainable and is going to have to change and change soon.

Middle class people everywhere across the country are greatly confused. First, there is justifiably a lot of confusion as to what or who constitutes the middle class. After all, in an effort to get votes, we've almost all been led to believe that we're in that group, even if we see ourselves to be in the upper or the lower end of the group. About the only people who can't be self-designated as part of that group are the truly very poor. There are a large number of people, though smaller than you would think, that truly are poor. All reasons aside, whether it be geographic, unfortunate circumstances beyond their control, medical or physical complications or restrictions, some people are just plain poor, and in a nation with earning capabilities as large as ours, there is just no reason why we can't bring enough relief to some who are less fortunate than us, to facilitate at least the perceived bare existence, comfort and dignity that American people have defined as fair and humane.

Keep in mind that, whatever level of support that may be, it assuredly far surpasses the life experienced by a large population of the rest of the world. Also, there is just no way that many, if not most of the poor should be under the illusion that they have anything coming, or are due any fair share, or for that matter, any help at all. The simple fact that we as a nation can help the truly needy should be enough reason why we do. There is surely a certain group of people who may have become needy, destitute, or incapable of providing for themselves while serving the rest of us, whether they be disabled veterans, or others serving in the line of duty. We have workmen's compensation systems in all states set up to provide for workers who are permanently or partially disabled while working. These benefits are provided and paid for, in most cases, by the employers and the employees. In many cases, the very people who were born with learning disabilities, or handicaps, are the least demanding and the most appreciative of any help received.

Then there are the rest of us. Just how many people truly realize or appreciate what came before them? What was simply here when they arrived, whether they were born or immigrated here? There are millions of Americans who complain about taxes or the way our government operates, many of whom are unaware or unwilling to admit that they don't even come close to contributing their fair share, if any at all. Of the roughly 50% of the people who pay no taxes at all, many are the people working or living right beside you, and wake up people, you may be included in this group. **Many people work, take home their paychecks, notice and complain about the taxes deducted from their check, just to receive a full refund if not more early the next year.**

But enough for now about what we contribute, how about what we receive? When my mother was still with us, after Dad passed away, my brothers, sister and I would stop by to visit at least every other day or so. There was always hot coffee and conversation. Mom and Dad had certainly not been rich but they had saved and lived very frugally all of their lives, not much different than most people of that generation. They saved, avoided debt, and never expected someone else to take care of them. They opted for the survivorship election for their social security benefits, receiving a lesser amount while they were both alive, in an effort to better provide for the one that remained, which turned out to be Mom. They had their home paid off decades earlier, had some modest investments, and some savings. Mom was left alone, but more than adequately provided for through the efforts, work, and lifestyle they put forth over a lifetime.

Not everyone of their generation did quite the same. I would sit and have coffee with Mom, and she would talk about world events and inevitably things would come around to politics, taxes, etc. One day I had to stop Mom and tell her that although she and Dad had paid in all of their life and contributed possibly more than their fair share, she was no longer paying anything. She was now receiving all of those benefits and then some. But as I explained, it was not only the social security dollars or Medicare services; I reminded her of the entire infrastructure that was presently serving her. She was never in disagreement with what I was explaining, and seemed to agree. It was just that back then we all had become accustomed to complaining about taxes and inefficient government. Most people rarely give any thought to – much less admit any responsibility or appreciation for—the thousands of things that are in place, taken care of for us every day, 24 hours a day to insure our safety, comfort, and wellbeing.

We could start by recognizing the need for government, as wasteful and inefficient as it may be, we have a system setup by our Founding Fathers that has proven over and over to be the best bad system on Earth. We can certainly point out its faults, but it truly is better than anything established elsewhere. It is set up with the means of being forever sustainable, able to adjust and amend for the undeterminable changes that have come up in the past and are still to come. **After more than two centuries in existence, it is an awful and embarrassing realization that our generation may have singlehandedly run this nation over the tipping point of being beyond repair.** There may be very few, if any of us that can excuse ourselves at least in some part for the destruction and damage we've either created or allowed. The nation's debt alone may lead to the complete downfall of the United States of America. I doubt that there is an adult person in this nation who has not been the recipient of great benefits, and very few if any who have adequately reciprocated to the extent they've received. We complain about stimulus, and rightfully so, but we fail to acknowledge that nearly every one of us has personally benefited, at least temporarily, whether it be through continued employment, a recovering stock market, or tamed inflation and the ability to still go down to the market or the gas pump and afford to continue on as usual.

Who pays for the great military force we have at our disposal? I'll be the first one to say that having this mighty force for our protection doesn't mean that we have to put it to use as much as we've done recently, if ever. One of the greatest and yet worst functions of our country's system is the right to vote. The sad thing about our right to vote, and for that matter our entire political system, is that today it seems to be broken. Almost every level of government seems to be gridlocked, but what we don't think about is that the system was set up in anticipation of times like this, and since the birth of this nation, there have been numerous times when things were at a similar point and people thought certain problems couldn't be overcome. Yet, a few years down the road, we're back to a working system, newly elected leaders, etc. **Leaders is the key word** in the last sentence, as for some time now **the American people have been electing anyone who may promise them whatever they want to hear**, rather than people who can actually lead. Media is a good thing in the sense that it allows regular people to become educated on what's going on around the world, as well as inside our government. However, the media has also injected exorbitant amounts of money to sway elections and issues.

I may not always be able to elect the person that I feel will be the best steward of our military, treasury, Constitution and Bill of Rights. Sometimes I am not even offered a good option and have only the option to vote for the best of the worst. The best leaders that we could get into office would be the ones with the diplomacy to keep us out of conflicts, yet the strength and backbone to show our might without ever having to use it. This goes way beyond our military, but extends to every aspect of governing our great nation. We need individuals who will step forward and fight for the things that are good for the future of our nation, even though these things may not be popular to the Hoggy Hogs who have the ability to vote them out. **This will take true leadership, the likes of which we have not seen rise to the top for a long time now.**

Who pays for the services that we never see, such as intelligence gathering, flight control, satellite, and space control? In this day and age, we can no longer pretend that our geographical borders are our only concern. Being this big and powerful nation, we have a big target on our back and we better have some presence not only around the world, but literally surrounding the world, in space. If we don't, they will. Our country has erred immensely by not only getting involved but, in many if not most cases, initiating conflicts abroad for many decades now. I doubt that there are more than a handful of people, and certainly not me, that are qualified to answer whether the United States should have been involved at all or to the extent that we have been in any of the military actions beginning with Korea, certainly Vietnam, and all the way up to today's activity in the Middle East. After all, we elect our leaders, and the leaders we, the American people elected made their decisions, good or bad, right or wrong, so who can we blame when or if we don't agree?

By my observations, it seems as if the American people are generally supportive of our government's operations as long as we're winning. When the first President Bush sent our military to Iraq, got in and out in a flash, publicizing the greatest trade show in history for our arms manufacturers on CNN, the United States showed its might and overwhelming strength to the rest of the world. Then he pulled us out. The nation's people loved it. Wow, we're tough, we're mighty, and no one dare mess with us. That's what people were thinking. Everyone likes to believe that we're the biggest, strongest, and most untouchable nation. Heck, if asked, a large chunk of the American people would tell you that we won the Vietnam War. Not only that, we're now a nation of people who live our lives satisfying a hunger for instant gratification, so we the people don't have a stomach for long drawn out conflicts. When George W. Bush got us involved in Iraq once again, it wasn't the same as his father's in-and-out operation. If any one were to look back at how we initially got involved in Vietnam, it was very similar. There simply was no exit plan, and as a result the U.S. had troops involved for over a decade. Jump forward to our Iraq and Afghanistan involvements, and both have very similar timeframes as well as outcomes. A big difference is that back in the 1960s and 1970s there were constantly protesters in the street, and the American people made their voices heard. Our more recent and ongoing messes seem to be things we all knew were happening as we just went on about our lives. Maybe the difference stems from the fact that we now have an all-volunteer military as opposed to back in the Vietnam era, when they were dragging our kids out of high school and forcing them to fight. But maybe the big difference today is that such a large percentage of our people just want to keep their head down and keep collecting their handouts; nobody wants anything to change.

I think many of us could debate for hours or days about the right or wrong of our past and present actions, but the one thing we all just assume, is that someone is out there looking after us. Though I will, without a doubt, be at the top of the list of those questioning our tactics, whether they be American military actions or supporting of groups around the world who are battling regimes that could bring harm to us, the one thing we should all agree on is that we can't just do nothing, and we should have a large and ready military presence, not only here but around the world, which is essential to our safety and survival. There are people in this country that just want to shrink and shrink that military and intelligence machine. I would just love it if that were possible, but maybe we could look at it like life insurance or fire insurance, in that we keep paying for it and keep it active and hope that we never need it. Is that a waste of money? I don't think so.

To put it plainly, there has never been a time in the history of this country when it has been more important to be prepared. I'm not just speaking about the obvious terrorist groups that we're all aware of, or more importantly, the ones we're not aware of, but I'm talking about nearly every nation around the globe. Wake up people: we are not the only smart ones, not the only ones with computers, missiles, and biological capabilities. When Japan invaded Pearl Harbor such a short time ago, they didn't choose Pearl Harbor only because we had an entire fleet of Navy ships parked and vulnerable; they also chose that target because at the time, they really didn't have the capability to reach much farther.

Today, most of us sit comfortably in our homes or go about our day with the misguided confidence that our nation is far superior and so strong that no other country or group would dare, or certainly would not be successful, in attacking us on our soil. After all, not an American alive has witnessed a war fought on our soil, but today it stands as a real and probable threat.

So, how much are you and I paying for that service? Some of us may pay a monthly payment for our home security company to monitor the door and window openings of our home. We don't have a problem paying to keep some thug from coming in and stealing our stuff, but just how much would we or should we be paying for a security monitoring system for our community and country? And then, not if, but when the alarm sounds and our nation is under attack, what would you or I pay to be adequately protected, whether it be our city, utility grid system, financial system under attack or some kind of known or unknown type of chemical or biological attack? Isn't it nice to know that someone pre-emptively thought about these happenings and had some sort of plan in place, some sort of emergency preparedness operation immediately in action? How many dollars is this worth? How much is each one of us paying, or how much should we be paying for this security? Unfortunately, more than any time in the history of this country, almost everything that has been provided for us, from military might down to daycare services, from bank and corporation bailouts to food stamps and housing has been purchased and paid for on credit. In other words, **we have not been paying our way**. Every one of us, well at least 99% of us have been getting far more in benefits than we've paid for. Not only has the typical American citizen spent the last couple of decades living beyond their means, enjoying today with little thought about tomorrow, our federal, state and local governments have been providing us with whatever will get our votes without getting compensation in return, simply by running up trillions of dollars in debt. Now, who do we suppose is ultimately going to pay off that debt?

Since most people are paying no taxes at all or only a little (but nowhere near what it takes to adequately pay for even a fraction of some of the things were talking about here), one would hope that someone is paying in to keep this system going. The poor are not paying for these things, and the middle class are not paying for these things. The answer is the rich. The very people who are under fire, who we're told are not paying their fair share, continue to pay for pretty much everything while the rest of the nation pretty much lives life without contributing. And even still, it cannot possibly be paid for by this small but wealthy group, so debt continues to soar, every day more than the last.

Though it changes from year to year, the top 10% of earners pay approximately 71% of the taxes collected. Now don't confuse this with paying the costs. The costs of most, if not all of the services we're talking about here are not paid, because the government is still borrowing most of the money that goes to paying for government services and, for the most part, the revenue being collected pays but soon will not pay for the interest on the debt we as a country are accumulating. The top 1% of earners pay 37% of the revenue collected, while the bottom 50% of earners, yes, the entire bottom half contribute collectively 2% of all federal income tax all revenue.

So we're told that those dirty rotten rich people that are essentially paying everybody else's way, that are pretty much picking up the entire bill must be making too much, right? Well, just imagine, what would happen if those rich people didn't make that much next year? What if they just took next year off and sat on the beach? The government is not going to stop spending money. They are not even going to spend less. They've already shown that they're incapable of doing that. No, they're going to continue to borrow more, spend more and eventually, in fact starting right now, they're going to begin extracting more and more from the very people who they are telling us have been taken advantage of, the middle class. But before they do that, before they send each one of you your bill, you can bet they're first going to go to the polls and charts to determine which groups of voters they least want to alienate. Since 50% of the people, each one individually worth one vote, many of whom are either Hoggy Hogs or just plain poor; collectively account for 50% of voters, it seems like a no brainer that they would do what has been so successful in the past. They will promise them more free stuff, solidify their votes, and leave the rest of us to foot the bill.

At this point, one may start to wonder, 'Hmm, if the rich were to stop earning and paying close if not more than half of everything they've earned, and another 50% of the tax filers are going to continue to pay virtually nothing, well then just who is going to be left to pick up the difference?'

Come on people, do we really want the high earners of this nation to make less? For that matter, do we really want anyone in this nation to earn less? Will someone, or anyone in the nation making less cause anyone else in the nation to make more? The answer is absolutely not, in fact, quite the opposite. The fact is that the overwhelming bulk of the high earners, the people who pay the majority of the taxes, are business owners, mostly small business owners and other self-employed people. Another fact is that the overwhelming majority of them are employers. An additional fact is that, not only are they employers, they are job creators, meaning they are people who have started a business or grown a businesses, many times one job at a time. Some facts are just too unbelievable to hear but here it goes.

As each employer painstakingly, usually while risking everything they've worked for, squeezes out enough profit (which is what companies are supposed to do in order to continue) to the point that they can add one or more jobs, they do so only with the expectation that they are able to earn additional income, otherwise, why would they go to that trouble and risk? So, if they beat the odds and are successful, they will earn more and as a result will pay more tax. Each time they enlarge their payroll, and assumedly earn more, they will pay more until one day they have enough employees—and subsequent earnings— that they will now pay nearly half if not more in income taxes. There is actually an overwhelming disincentive to build that business and add employees.

So, if this individual were to not create the jobs, who will? **Jobs, isn't that the one thing missing?**

Wouldn't many of this nation's troubles simply evaporate if we could create a job for everyone who was capable of working?" I intentionally avoided saying "a job for everyone who wanted one" because until we change the path our country is going down of making it too easy on the Hoggy Hogs, it will continue to be just too easy not to work and to not contribute.

So, how much is fair? I'm not talking about how much is fair for any particular person to earn. The American people have been brainwashed for the last six years into thinking that it is wrong for someone to make a lot of money or to become successful. Guess what? High earning, financially successful people are not Hoggy Hogs, no they are quite the opposite since they carry the majority of the load to support the millions (and growing number) of Hoggy Hogs who are enjoying the free ride. What is the fair share that a typical high earner, an employer, the average one-percenter should pay in income tax? First we'll examine just what they are paying;

Top 1% of American Earners

Average Taxable Income:	$ 1.4 million
Average 2013 Federal Income Tax Bill:	$507,000
2013 Marginal Tax Rate:	39.6 %

It has become politically popular to brainwash everyone who is not a member of the top one percent of earners (coincidentally 99% of the voters) to think that the 1% not only makes too much, but that they don't pay their fair share.

At least for now, let's not examine all of the 10% top earners that pay 71% of all taxes, many of whom may be your friends or neighbors. Instead, let's look at the 1% that pay 37% of the taxes, that's over one-third of all taxes collected. An average one-percenter that earns a taxable income of $1.4 is most likely a small business owner, maybe your boss or possibly the owner of the company employing one of my children or yours. At the end of the year, after paying all the countless taxes and fees to local and state government agencies, the boss earns 1.4 million dollars. Since the IRS wants their money sooner rather than later, the boss has sent in his tax payments each quarter, every three months, in the amount of $126,750 for a total of $507,000. I have to wonder, if we were to introduce a hundred people to this boss, educate them just a little about the history of the company, what they do, a little about the lives of the employees, just a quick lesson on what that company and that boss contribute to the community and overall society, how many of those one-hundred people would think that the company owner is paying his fair share, just enough, or how many would think that he should pay less or more? How many would look at that figure, over a half million dollars and say something like, "Man that just doesn't seem right?"

No, I can't believe that most people, if they took five minutes to educate themselves, would believe that the high earners are not paying at least their fair share. So, is the problem that they don't want someone else to make more than them? Could the real problem be that they feel that they should make the same as those high earners, maybe that everyone in the nation should make the same amount, regardless of effort, or capabilities?

Now, if a community organizer with high ambitions can convince most of the voters that they're not getting their fair share and that he can fix that, isn't he pretty much assured to get elected? Then maybe, just for good measure, he promises 50% of the voters that they not only are going to have to pay nothing in taxes, but he's going to give them free stuff, and lots of it. But just in case, just on the outside chance that there are still too many level-headed people left in the nation that wouldn't be sold a cure-all serum off a wagon from a traveling flim-flam man, he feeds on an illusion that the bulk of the people had already begun to believe, in that the recent bout of prosperity had been real and in fact it was the norm, **something to which every middle class person was entitled**. Throw in a promise to assure every person in the country full healthcare, all 320 million plus, and that ought to just about clench the election.

Boy! If I'm in a supermarket parking lot and some guy comes up to me, opens the trunk of his car and offers to sell me $2,500 worth of new stereo equipment, still in the boxes for $200, and I blindly hand over the cash then find that I have purchased empty boxes, I guess I kind of deserve what I got: empty promises. Perhaps, just maybe, had I asked a question or two of this parking lot salesman, my limited bit of common sense would have kicked in and I'd of kicked this guy to the curb.

Not all of our elected leaders are bad people. There is quite possibly not a one of them that wouldn't have figured out a way years ago to just give health care to every person who calls America their home, except, of course, for one minor detail. No one has thus far been able to figure out how they could even come close to being able to pay for it.

Too many people believed what they wanted to hear and never demanded an answer of the community organizer who was going to give them everything, **to one simple question: How?** These are just some of the fallacies that the American people, ready for "change," fell prey to. Has most of the nation lost the ability to think or reason, or have they simply gotten lazy?

HEALTH CARE HAS BEEN REDEFINED

I've often thought that if I were a high ranking political figure, I could fix almost all of the problems this nation is experiencing. Realizing that surely there are countless others in office today with good intentions as well as great ideas, it seems that what's truly missing is leadership, and it is missing in most levels of our government today. Most of the problems we face today haven't developed overnight and most will take even longer to straighten out, but like most things, you can only get to that destination once you're headed down the right road in the proper direction. For far too long, we've been heading in the completely wrong direction and with no one with the guts to speak up and turn us around.

Though the country's problems may seem complicated and difficult, as most things, generally the solution is simple, but not easy;

simple, but not quick. Almost any problem that the nation is experiencing can be compared to a household or a business dilemma. For instance, if a household or a business is spending more than it is taking in for an indefinite period of time, it simply has two and only two choices.

Either the household or business must spend less or bring in more. In either case, tough choices and unpopular decisions must be made, and with each day that passes without these corrections, the task gets much tougher. In the case of a household, there must be a leader, generally either the mother or father of the family. The leader will not be popular with the rest of the family when he or she starts taking away all the things that other family members have become so accustomed to, the very things that have made up their lifestyle, in most cases, for their entire lives. These family members have never put much thought into where these things came from since they've just always been there. Most have considered themselves to be middle class people in America and, well, 'everybody lives like this, don't they?' So, whether it's the expensive cable TV or internet package, or the gym membership with personal trainers, the dance classes, sports shoes and uniforms, trips to the hair or tanning salon, expensive birthday parties, vacations, possibly the house that is larger than they can afford, or going back to driving a 10-year-old car instead of the two new ones in the garage, there are sure to be some upset people and the leader of the family is going to be very unpopular for a while. Thankfully, the family leader can't be voted out of the family, and frankly, this is the very reason they just may succeed. The second option for this family is to bring in more revenue, maybe by working additional hours, getting a better paying job, or possibly a second job. If the problem has gone on and has been ignored too long, the solution will probably require both cost cutting as well as additional revenue.

DON'T FEED THE SQUIRRELS

In the case of a business, pretty much the same thing has to happen. Cut expenses, raise more revenue, or in contrast to the family unit, there is always the option of simply going out of business. Both households and businesses can consider bankruptcy if the situation is too far gone. Should the family go bankrupt, when they are through, they will still be there as a family. They will live another day. They will be able to start the next day and hopefully, depending upon the leadership of the family unit, start again, not over promise or overspend, and do just fine.

The government, having the same first two options, must do the same thing. The longer the problem is allowed to grow, the tougher the consequences and the longer it will take to work through the tough times. Would the best solution be to spend less, bring in more revenue, or both? The government cannot go out of business. Why? Because come the next day, there would still be this nation in need of a government; the problems would still be there. But could it go bankrupt? The term being fed to us in preparation for this feared event is *default*. Every scenario involving our government defaulting on its debt is complicated and very ugly. We're not only talking about debt, but defaulting on obligations, or promises, and total destruction of everything we know. We certainly don't want to think about that, but that certainly appears to be more and more likely, even imminent.

One great leader, that's all we really need, one that will make the tough choices instead of lying to the gullible American people and kicking the can down the road for the next guy to worry about.

Another problem that the government faces when attempting to spend less is that so much of the economy we have come to see as normal is dependent upon government spending or stimulus. People associate the word stimulus with government bailouts of the banks and such. The fact is that the majority of business, as well as the resulting jobs, have been either subsidized or propped up by government money or guarantees. So many individuals and businesses have been at the trough, essentially getting their handouts, and possibly unaware of this fact. A large share of U.S. commerce today would not be happening if it were not for government spending and therefore government borrowing.

Each one of the problems that our politicians have kicked down the road can be reduced, improved upon, and with time, turned around. It would assuredly take decades of sacrifice and lowered expectations by the entire nation, but with the proper leadership, it would be possible to deal with everything from the national debt, poverty and unemployment, to immigration, just to mention a few.

Healthcare, however, is not solvable, at least not to the extent that it has been promised and to the extent expected from the American people today. You see, people now have it in their minds that every person in the nation is entitled to the same great medical system, in its entirety, without regard to who or how it is to be paid for. After all, that's what they've been promised. The question has certainly been brought up, but the people hear what they want to hear: FREE STUFF.

People just want to avoid the question: HOW TO PAY FOR IT?

Thirty years ago, a trip to the doctor consisted of looking in your ear, tapping on your knee, and maybe checking the sound of a cough, while the doc touched you in your privates. This country and the entire world has made great advancements in the medical field. We have imaging, scanning, joint and organ replacement, drug development, gene research and therapy. We're very close to a point theoretically of being able to keep a person alive indefinitely. There is one problem. We've gotten so good that people are living a lot longer. People used to be pretty trouble free until they got up to about age sixty, when they often got sick and died. The medical community didn't keep prolonging their lives very long, they just died. Now, nearly any person from sixty on, an age where they in past years would have not even been here, has at their disposal almost unlimited services that a few decades ago were unimaginable. Furthermore, every person alive today has spent their life eating processed foods, living in a polluted environment, not to mention in many cases eating or drinking too much and smoking. To add to the problems, many have been gorging on medications to the point that they are dependent on them. With all the bad things we've been putting into our body and lungs, we're developing serious problems earlier, yet thanks to our miraculous medical system, we're being kept alive longer.

The medical progress that has been made in recent years is nothing short of amazing. Along the way medicine has been responsible for a lot of jobs in areas from research and development to the implementation of the latest amazing advancements. Enormous amounts of money have been spent and made, and we seem to be nowhere close to an end of the advancement or discovery. Many individuals have invested their 401(k) savings into the companies that are creating and discovering these new developments, from drug companies to hip and knee manufacturers, and many have profited handsomely. But like all great things, this doesn't come without a price. It costs enormous amounts of money to develop a new drug. People gripe and complain about the drug companies making too much money, etc. Well, I say that if they were not allowed to make a profit, we would have none of these advancements.

Through the amazing services and procedures available today, a person can find themselves hospitalized for something that a few years ago would have killed them, and they can walk out cured. The other side of this coin is that they will have run up bills easily into the hundreds of thousands if not millions of dollars. If this were limited to a few people, the costs could be absorbed by the rest. But no, the fact is, with all of us living so much longer, short of being hit and killed by a bus, most people will rack up more medical costs then they may have earned in their entire life. This may stem from a one-time event, such as an accident or cancer, or it may add up over the years due to their treatment for diabetes, high blood pressure or arthritis. The fact is, the longer each person lives the more likely they are to need an operation or replacement on a joint or organ.

If each person, on average, is likely to receive more services then they are possibly able to pay for, it doesn't take anyone smarter than an idiot to see that it's not going to work! With half of the people being promised first rate care without paying a cent and another large group being promised a partial subsidy by the government (again, borrowed money) there are just a few left to foot the whole bill. And you guessed it! Once again, it's those dirty rotten rich people that are expected to pay the bill.

I suppose we will again go to the dirty rotten rich and make them pay for everyone else, except that this is so big and involves so much money that we could not only take everything that the wealthy earn, but we could literally take all that they have, and it will still not be enough to fulfill the healthcare promises made and expected. Oh, and don't forget that the dirty rotten rich are, or at least were the employers, which may not last if everything is taken from them and the jobs are gone.

Wake up people! Where do you think the jobs have been going? What do you think has been happening?

Right now we've got the largest group ever at or coming to retirement age. They are about to require an immense amount of medical care. We have a generation of children coming up inactive and obese, almost guaranteeing that they will require far more help than previous generations. We've got the bulk of the rest of the nation who are sitting around and not working because it's easier to just take handouts, or maybe they are working, but are so accustomed to living in this nation without paying their way that they just expect they will get everything promised to them.

This great health care machine is similar to a bridge built to nowhere. What if a company was to go out and do all the expensive development to create a space shuttle, an amazing creation, and then they decided to go and build enough space shuttles to provide one for every person in every household across America? They put these shuttles out on the space shuttle lot for sale and wait for them to sell. Not a good business plan. But maybe if they were to contribute enough money to the community organizer's election campaign, he, being a pretty good salesman, could promise each American a space shuttle parked in every driveway. The system seems to work, until it doesn't. No, it is no more possible for the entire health care system to be offered and available to every person in the country than it would be to give them each a space shuttle. At least with the space shuttle it would be a onetime expense, as opposed to the need for expensive health care that will only continue to grow larger and more expensive.

The answer that no one wants to hear, plain and simple, is that some are going to have to go without, or at the very least, **many of the now-promised and expected services are going to have to be limited**.

Being in the building industry, I've seen firsthand that the Hoggy Hog people getting free housing are, in many cases, living in better housing than the hard working people building the structures. I've been there after the lazy Hoggy Hogs get up at about 9:30 in the morning and go out and start their day, fishing, smoking, or whatever else they do since they're not working. Our workers have been up since dawn, rain or shine, and at the end of the pay period wonder why the dollars missing from their check are going to make the Hoggy Hogs' lives easier.

We see the same thing at the grocery store when the Hoggy Hogs are purchasing food that many of us would not or cannot buy, and they're doing it with money they didn't earn. Would it be inhumane or simply too politically incorrect if we were to instead provide a simple roof over their head and the basics of food to survive? Why not eliminate our food stamp programs and start providing basic healthy ingredients, such as rice, vegetables, and flour. Why provide new housing with multiple bathrooms and instead create some 8x10 concrete block structures with a community shared toilet area at the end of the building. I guarantee that we would see a lot more motivation for those chronically unemployed recipients to go out and begin a life of contributing to society instead of a lifetime of taking. We provide public bus transportation to supply a basic need for people without a car. We don't supply them each with a Cadillac Escalade, though that may be an idea for Barack Obama if he were to be able to run for another term.

BACK WHEN INSURANCE WAS INSURANCE

Pre-existing conditions or not, smoker or 200 lbs. overweight, no one has ever been uninsurable. Insurance was always available to any of us, of course based on our own individual risk factors.

Many people just don't understand what insurance is and how a typical insurance company has always operated, for hundreds of years, in fact up until now. People love to hate insurance companies until the day they experience a loss or disaster and the company has their back. Whether it is home owners, auto, medical or life insurance, we pay the monthly premiums and hope we never need it. The best thing that could happen to each of us is to pay the premiums our entire life and never get anything in return. Most of us, especially in our younger years, don't have adequate savings to properly care for our surviving spouse or family in the event of our early death, so we purchase life insurance. We could probably afford to go to the doctor for a minor medical problem and pay for it ourselves along with a simple one-time prescription, but what we worry about is that major illness or accident that may rack up massive bills, so medical insurance seems like a necessity. Same thing goes for auto insurance. Generally, if you can easily afford to suffer a specific loss, you probably shouldn't pay to insure it.

Insurance companies are just that, companies. They are in business to earn a reasonable profit and to stay in business. If they did not earn enough to stay in business, then they would not be there for you and me when the time comes that we need them. This is no different than any other type of business. If they were to overcharge for their offering, people would simply choose not to do business with them and would go with their competitor. In fact, up until recently, the insurance business has been very competitive. We as consumers love that; we love businesses being very competitive to earn our business. The truth is that insurance companies may not even make a dime off our premiums, in that they very well may pay out as much or more than we pay them on average. Where they make their money is by using and investing our premium dollars between the time we pay them and the time when we suffer a loss and submit a claim.

We may pay auto insurance for ten years without an accident or claim and then one day we rear end the car ahead of us and they take care of us. What they have been doing during that period of time is earning interest and investment income off of the dollars we've been paying them. That seems like a pretty good deal, since we get what we bargained for and they have been able to earn enough money along the way to assure that they are there for us when we need them.

This was working very well for everyone back before interest rates were artificially lowered to nearly zero by the Federal Reserve System. But throw in a couple of steep down turns in the stock market and suddenly they can't earn their living off the time difference between our payment of premiums and our claims. That's to some degree why we've seen significant increases in insurance premiums in recent years. These are indirect consequences which stem from the government's manipulating of interest rates. Of course there are other reasons for increased rates. The cost to repair the cars of today is far more than it was with older models. Obviously the cost of repairing our human body is far more than in past years simply because we have so much more available than we did.

When applying for auto insurance, as we all should expect, the company is going to pull up your driving record. If you've got a string of speeding tickets, multiple accidents, and a drunken driving conviction, it stands to reason that in the eyes of the insurance company, you present a much larger risk than a person with a perfect record. The company is also going to take into consideration how long of a commute you have and how many miles you typically drive in a year. I think we can all understand that the risk is higher for a person who drives 40,000 miles as opposed to one who drives 20,000. Another thing they may consider is your location and whether you drive rural roads or city streets. Statistics show that from one city to another, the cost of collision repairs and medical claims vary significantly. If I happen to be a safe driver that has shown a history of good behavior and I am less of a risk to the insurer, I should expect to receive the "safe driver" rates, and **I certainly shouldn't have to pay for others' recklessness or bad decisions**.

Now, when we sit down with a life insurance salesman, we'll have to disclose our medical history, whether we smoke or have ever smoked. They'll want to know our weight to determine the likelihood of future health problems, and they may even require us to have a physical examination. Just like statistics show that a sixteen -year-old driver is likely to cost significantly more in claims than someone who is thirty, a smoker or someone who is overweight or a heavy drinker may still qualify for a policy but at a higher rate, relative to the higher risk and greater likelihood of incurred costs. Again, if I happen to be a non-smoking, healthy-eating individual I should expect to receive the lower non-smoker rate. Even most of the higher risk people can understand that they pose more risk and have no choice but to pay the higher price. The smoking or overeating is the result of continuous decisions made and the individual should not be subsidized by the rest of us who have chosen to make better decisions. When it comes to a driving record, sometimes high premiums may be the result of poor decisions, reckless behavior, or maybe a person is just not a good driver. That person may not be good at baseball, football, or driving. He or she may just be uncoordinated. We've all seen people who just aren't good at a lot of things. In some cases, a person may just have plain been unlucky and wound up at the wrong place at the wrong time, resulting in a bad collision and a riskier looking record. Most people, whether it be the good or bad driver, the clean living, healthy individual or the one who has abused his or her body, understand why the rates charged to each of them should be directly related to the risk they impose, whether it be in the form of lower or higher rates. **Generally, even the highest risk driver can still purchase auto insurance but at a much higher rate, commonly known as *high-risk insurance*.** There are still several companies competing for that driver's business, just at a higher rate.

Over the years, insurance companies have nearly perfected the art of determining the proper risk for the sixteen-year-old driver or the unhealthy, smoking overeater through actuarial tables. The cost may not exactly match a particular individual, but on average they've proved to be near perfect. None of us want to live the good clean life, practice good decision making, just to end up paying the bill for the people who choose to spend their money on cigarettes and eat their meals at McDonalds.

We've all heard of people being turned down for medical insurance due to pre-existing conditions. Normally this is just not the case. No different than the driver with a drunken or poor driving record that may have no choice other than risk insurance, **almost anyone in any condition can purchase coverage, but at a price that matches their particular situation and risk**. The companies have this figured out and they are good at it. The only way that they can offer the proper price to the low risk customer is to charge the proper risk premium to the higher risk customer as well. There is an insurance policy available for almost anything or anyone but it may be expensive or have some limitations. A policy can be purchased for a home situated in a floodway that has a history of flood damage, but at a much higher rate than the home in an area not prone to flooding. Insurance companies have maps for every foot of the country and they know the risk and the appropriate premium to charge. We don't expect to have to pay for the person that chooses to stay in that flood prone area any more than we should expect that the insurance company should be forced to enter into a contractual agreement with the high risk individual at a price where they will likely lose money.

That was then, this is now. President Obama shoved the Affordable Care Act, which basically tells insurance companies that they have to accept the smoker or junk food junkie and charge them no more than the healthy living person, down the throats of American citizens. President Obama, a smoker, has never been in business, constantly talks down business as if it is the enemy, and has done everything in his power to convince the American people that business is bad. He doesn't think that an insurance company should be able to offer a competitive price for medical insurance to me as a non-smoker. He thinks an insurance company, a private for-profit company should have to accept a person in any condition, with any known problems and risks and not charge them any more than the person with low risk. It does not take a genius to figure out that the only way to do that is to charge everyone else more, and as it turns out, significantly more. Then, hidden in the 2,700 page document that admittedly none of the lawmakers had a chance to read, they basically guarantee the insurance companies that, regardless of the claims they may incur, they are guaranteed to make the profit they expect. He then hid in that document that no one read, a ton of taxes to help pay for it so he could claim that the Affordable Care Act will pay for itself. When I refer to 2,700 pages, that is the reference you typically hear, but the truth is that to fully understand the Affordable Health Care Act, you may have to wade through more like 11,000 pages of laws. That would partially explain why Nancy Pelosi said, "We have to pass the bill so that you can find out what is in it."

Small business owners, that have been the salvation for our economy and have been responsible for the bulk of the job growth over the last two decades, once had some incentive to encourage employees to not smoke and act responsibly. We tried to hire the people who made good choices. By adding in all of the high risk people in the same pool as the clean living good choice makers, essentially now the employer offering medical insurance to their employees is hindered from the ability to continue to hire new or even retain the existing people. This is one of the clearest examples of *Job Killer Legislation*.

President Obama made a bad choice to smoke cigarettes for years. Why should he expect that the rest of us should pay for his bad choices?

Medical insurance companies are no longer insurance companies, and are now simply an outlet for the government socialistic flow of borrowed money. As far as medical insurance, insurance companies no longer serve a purpose.

I can completely understand and feel compassion when a certain individual suffers at no fault of their own, just plain bad luck or a raw deal. The fact is that if you choose to drive your car without comprehensive coverage, you made the conscious decision to take on that risk instead of paying a company to take the risk. Some people do the responsible thing and others don't. In most cases when we hear of a person or a family being debt-ridden or bankrupted by excessive medical bills or a onetime incident, it usually comes down to the fact that they were under-insured, or more likely uninsured. If a person chooses to drive without auto insurance, they are making the conscious decision to gamble that they won't suffer an accident. If they choose to gamble by living their life without or with inadequate medical insurance (often opting to spend those dollars on something else in their life), they should not expect the rest of us to be there to bail them out after we did the responsible thing and paid for our own coverage.

If someone smoked cigarettes, drove intoxicated, or just plain lived an un-healthy lifestyle, their insurance premiums would undoubtedly be quoted at a higher rate. So, the individual consciously decides not to pay those premiums, but instead to spend those dollars on more cigarettes, alcohol and junk food, in which case it's just a matter of time until someone else pays the price.

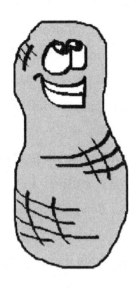

We've all sampled the HOODY!

I GUESS WE'D ALL DO A LOT OF THINGS DIFFERENTLY

We don't like to think about it because it can and would drive us crazy to think about every action, regardless of how meaningless, we have taken and will take; these choices, small and large, make up the life we're living today as well as our entire future. Something we did yesterday or decades ago not only changed our whole destiny but the destiny of others, including people we know and people we have never met or thought about. That time fifteen years ago you pushed the snooze button on the alarm clock or that yellow light you went through instead of stopping put you forever in a different place and time from that time forward. How about that time you were afraid to approach that person you may have been attracted to and may have gotten to know, possibly even married and had children with? Of course those children, as much as I'm sure you would love and be proud of them, are not the children you call your family today. For better or worse, it's crazy to think back and wonder 'what if?' If you ended up married to an awful person, had ugly children, created an unhappy life, you may certainly think back and wonder what could have been? The truth is turning right instead of left twenty years ago may be just one reason you now are living the life you see today. For all you know, had you turned left instead of right, putting you in a different place and time, you very well would today have a totally different circle of friends, different occupation, or maybe you would have crashed in the next intersection or years later, leaving you crippled or dead. The reality is that these and all other actions changed and will continue to change not only your entire life, but the lives of many other people from that time forward. The fact that you ended up having a child with the partner you did as opposed to any one of a million others out there is the reason that your child exists and another or others don't.

We've all heard a divorced person say something like, "The only good thing to come out of that marriage is my children." The truth is that it is not only our children we would not want to change. For most of us, there are a lot of things in our lives that we wouldn't want to change or have not to have happened. Sometimes people seem to get a bad break from actions that just don't seem to be their fault, however pretty much every action we took leading up to that change was a result of decisions we made throughout our lives. There is nearly nothing that couldn't or wouldn't have happened differently, good or bad, had we made different decisions just once or throughout our lives. Predominately, we all like to take credit for the good things, but it is rare that we want to take credit or responsibility for the decisions that led to anything negative or not to our liking.

Each time I go to a doctor the same questions will come up about family history, illnesses in the family, how long my parents lived. I have to say that I don't know the answers to all of these questions because everyone died young. My parents, grandparents, uncles and aunts, all of them, died of cancer or some smoking-related illness. I can't tell the doctor whether I expect to live to the usual family life span of 60 to 70 years, or since I've never smoked a cigarette, maybe I should expect to live to be 100.

But how about that person that we've all known who, out of the blue is diagnosed with some awful disease like cancer or multiple sclerosis and they seemed to be the person who lived the model life. They never smoked, seemed to eat right, exercised, yet they are stricken with something that just seems so unfair. Why them? How could this happen to a healthy person when it seems as though there are so many people who live such an unhealthy lifestyle, yet they're still here and kicking? We sometimes think we're doing all the right things just to find out later that something that seemed to be out of our control has been hurting us all along. Could their illness have been caused by something they have been eating or drinking or the environment in which they live or work? Maybe they've had a defective gene or genes in their body since birth. There was a time when expectant mothers would smoke or drink alcohol while pregnant and not think a thing about it. Maybe it was the fumes in the home due to the rubber-backed rugs in the living room where their mother would rock them as a baby.

There's possibly not a person alive who hasn't said or thought, 'Why am I so short?' or 'bald?' or 'Why am I not prettier?' The tall man is much more likely to be able to play professional basketball than the average or below average height individual. Though much of the obesity we see today is a result of lifestyle, there really are some young people who were born to large parents and are simply big-boned and will probably have a tougher time than others looking like those thin models on the cover of the magazines at every grocery store check stand. Some men are bald at thirty while others have a full head of hair all their life. These physical differences have always been around, yet only recently has it been drilled into us that things aren't fair.

We're being told that it isn't fair that Buck who has lived his entire life in backwoods Kentucky doesn't earn the same money or enjoy the same lifestyle as the wealthy software engineer Paul, working at Microsoft, or Steve, the stock broker working on Wall Street. Maybe that software engineer was born just down the hill from the guy who has lived his entire life in poverty, but the difference is that Paul got out. He finished high school, looked around the little town where he had spent his life and said, "**I want more**." The only girls he saw in his little town were Daisy May and Bobby Sue, neither of which were real beauties. Buck and Daisy May would sneak up to the hayloft time and time again until, who'd have thought, Daisy May was knocked up, and a new cycle began.

Bobby Sue had the hots for Paul but Paul had other things in mind, so he kept his zipper up. Boy, it sure looked like Buck and Daisy May were having a lot of fun there for a while. Paul looked at Bobby Sue and envisioned what their children would look like. He thought he could do better. Paul left town, got additional education, worked a number of jobs until he could land in the place that made him the happiest. Boy, it wasn't easy.

The whole time that Paul was going to college and working two part-time jobs, Buck and Daisy May were back in the hills of Kentucky doing what they were good at, having more kids, and going to the mailbox to collect their government checks. Buck would work when he could, but things were tough. Of course he wasn't working two jobs or studying like his old friend Paul, so he would pretty much spend his time drinking up his entire paycheck at the local bar. Poor Daisy May was pregnant in her junior year and never finished high school. She never did really learn any marketable skills so they relied solely on Buck's income, limited as it was. Buck and Daisy May both smoked, Daisy May about a pack a day, and Buck about two packs a day. Neither Buck or Daisy May were ever very good with numbers, so their paychecks and government checks just never really seemed to stretch, and they never were able to figure out that three packs of cigarettes per day, times 30 days, well that was somewhere around 90 packs each month. They did make some moves to keep those costs down by buying in bulk, by the carton, but usually they couldn't quite swing that whole carton so most of the time they would just buy 3 or 4 packs at the convenience store just to get by. When they did go to the grocery store, cigarettes were usually the first thing in the cart, even before food for the family. They had to be creative and careful when shopping since the government food stamps could only be used for food and not for tobacco or alcohol. Daisy May quickly figured out that if she went to the corner store where her old friend Bobby Sue worked as a clerk, they could simply ring up the smokes as a food item. She and Bobby Sue could even do some trading for the food stamps and generate some cash so she could purchase some lottery tickets and go to Friday night Bingo.

The whole time Buck and Daisy May were living their life, buying their loaded pizzas from the local pizza joint, receiving subsidized rent from the government, Paul was working two jobs, studying, and eating Top Ramen and Kraft Macaroni and Cheese. He spent most of his time through college either sharing a place to live with several people or crashing on someone's couch. One reason why Paul continued to work two jobs while going to school is that he didn't want to graduate with a bunch of debt. Those were some tough years. It wasn't until his third year in college when things got a little easier for Paul. While he was waiting tables on the weekend he met a co-worker, Julie, who was also nearing graduation and they started spending a lot of time together. As it turned out they had a lot in common, as she had come from a similar situation and had grown up in a very small town and just like Paul, she ventured out and had taken a chance at a better life.

Paul and Julie both put tremendous effort into their schooling, but even more importantly, they had prioritized their life, made a lot of little sacrifices along the way, and as they neared graduation, they both set out to seek employment in the same area since it was obvious they were going to spend the rest of their lives together. Each of them went directly from college and started new jobs in the Seattle area. But the work was not done. They each took positions with different companies, Paul in the technology field and Julie at a marketing firm. They had each worked jobs since they were young so they knew what it took to move into a new position and start at the bottom.

They soon married, took a four-day camping honeymoon and went right back to work. They were both working long hours and competing with other people who were equally energetic and talented. They soon found that the corporate life was no walk in the park, but after a couple of short years they each were able to show their strong work ethic and value and they were handsomely compensated and promoted.

Paul and Julie never really saw it coming or knew when their lives had changed so drastically but the lives they were experiencing in the

DON'T FEED THE SQUIRRELS

Seattle area looked nothing like what they had each respectively left behind in their old home towns. By this time they were living in a nice condo, driving decent cars, and dressing well. They had a great circle of friends, both from work as well as other married couples they had come to know. Unlike Buck and Daisy May, going out for pizza and beer with Buck spending his abundance of free time at the corner bar, Paul and Julie were finally able to experience fine dining and cocktails. In their free time Paul would golf or work out at the club, and Julie got into Yoga and tennis. The people that they associated with would typically dine on sushi or salads instead of the junk food Paul and Julie remembered as the usual fare for meal out back home. They had grown up in an atmosphere where almost everyone smoked, but now they don't know a person who is a smoker and rarely even see a person smoking.

Paul and Julie worked their way through college and at the age of 22, they had no debt but they also had no assets. They owned nothing except the clothes they were wearing. Their entire combined net worth was zero. Now Buck and Daisy May, on the other hand, had been very busy building their life and accumulating things. Daisy May was driving a late model SUV, and Buck had recently purchased a brand new pick-up truck. Two years earlier, Daisy May's daddy had passed away and left them the house that she had grown up in. It wasn't much more of a cabin or a shack. There had been no maintenance done on it in years, but hey, they were homeowners.

Buck may have figured it out a little late but he decided to get serious about work and he really stuck with one job until he got pretty good at it and was now working full time. In fact, he was so good at it that his boss put a lot of responsibility on him, paid him more and offered him a lot of overtime. With this new income, it seemed as though their mailbox was never empty. It seemed that everyone wanted to lend them money. They fixed up the old house, bought nice furnishings; they even built a shop out back to park the new boat, hunting gear, and other toys. They were living the good life. They were really enjoying this middle-income lifestyle. Every time they got something new or better they were moving up and pretty proud of the life they were building.

Unfortunately, though, they weren't alone. Some of their buddies around town were getting nice stuff, too. Even though they were enjoying things that a few short years ago they would have never even dreamed of, which should have made them feel rich, or at least happy, each time they got something new, it seemed that there was always a friend or neighbor that got something bigger or better. They would get together with friends and all the talk was vacations, early retirement, and how the value of their houses had gone up again.

Buck and Daisy May had purchased a new riding lawn mower and all new appliances, and got a great discount. All they had to do was open a credit card and pay easy installment payments. They quickly found that most everything could be purchased like that. Daisy May was driving the four children around in the shiny SUV, carrying her Coach handbag full of charge cards. They had everything they wanted, furniture, clothing, big screen TVs, you name it, and there seemed to be no limit. Boy, Buck seemed to have really provided for his family. Not only was Buck earning nearly $50,000 a year now with his overtime and all, it seemed that every time they turned around, the old house had gone up in value. Three times in a period of three years, they refinanced the house. How could they not? Interest rates were continually going lower, and the appraiser would tell them that they could borrow so much more. They were continually able to draw out cash, pay down the balance on some of their credit cards, and start the process all over again. Not only was Buck a great hard-working provider, it seemed as though Daisy May was a financial genius.

Buck never really knew what was happening but when he'd come home and Daisy May would tell him that she just got the interest rate lowered on their home again, how could that be a bad thing?

So we all know the rest of the story about Buck, Daisy May, Paul and Julie. At 22 years old, Paul and Julie didn't own a thing. They didn't have a penny to their name. Buck and Daisy May, however, seemed to have it all figured out. They were living the typical middle class American life and seemed to have it all. The only problem is that **it was not real**. Paul and Julie were worth zero, but they were so much better off than the friends they had left behind. Buck and Daisy May would spend the rest of their lives paying for the things they purchased years ago and had long since worn out. They were poverty stricken "big time" but they didn't even know it. Most of their friends were in about the same shape, destined to spend the rest of their days living in poverty and complaining about how unfair it is. They all owed more money on their homes then they were ever really worth, even at the peak. Now that the real estate market had corrected, they were all basically screwed. Everything in their house, garage, or on their backs had been either charged or purchased with borrowed money. This was not just Buck and Daisy May who had made bad decisions and gorged on all the instant gratification available, it was everyone they knew, the whole community. Sadly, throw a dart at a map of the entire country and you would see pretty much the same thing. It was either or. Either the Buck and Daisy Mays, or the Paul and Julies, those that for a short time were the *haves and the have-nots* would forever thereafter be the *have-nots and the haves*. Yeah, the rest of their story goes like this:

The Paul and Julie's of the world, who made the better decisions, didn't live like gluttonous pigs, and worked hard and provided for themselves went on to buy things when they could afford them, raise their families responsibly, and become self-sufficient contributors to our great country. After a very short time of sacrificing and hard work, they would spend their lives at least living a pretty good life. Their only downside is that they've now got the rest of the nation, the bulk of the people, the Buck and Daisy Mays to support. And boy! The Buck and Daisy Mays, they have tasted the good life, and yet if they were to be asked, in fact if most of the nation were to be asked, they'd say "It's not fair!" and, "We're not getting a fair shake." What about income equality, why do some people make so much more than them? Not only that, after years of smoking, drinking, and eating loaded pizzas, their health is failing, but fortunately there are still enough innovative hard working people in this country who have developed amazing drugs and medical procedures to keep all the Hoggy Hogs alive and supplied with new joints, prescription drugs, and organs. And now it seems that many Americans, the bulk of them either Hoggy Hogs or non-contributors, can't imagine going back to living the life they earned, or didn't earn to be more exact; they want to continue on with the same high standard of living that the Bucks and Daisy Mays became accustomed to.

What should be seen as obvious can go a lifetime without being realized. Unless the Bucks and Daisy Mays of this country change the types of decisions they are making and their actions, their life will just continue to get harder, and in their eyes seem more and more unfair, when at the same time Paul and Julie will most likely continue to enjoy the benefits of their decisions and life will just get easier and more enjoyable.

Sometimes, however, even the people who are succeeding and making all the right decisions can derail themselves. Generally this happens because they simply don't appreciate what they have, and what they've created, or the life they've built. One thing that holds true with almost anyone in nearly any situation is that **if you can't appreciate what you've got, you can never really enjoy it**. Take your marriage or partner, your children, job, friends or possessions, the more appreciation you realize, the more you will enjoy them. The more you enjoy them, the better you will treat them, the more you will want to be around them, the more appreciation you will have and show them, until each is continuously reciprocated. Whether it is a marriage or a job, the more you give, the more you will receive, guaranteed. Provided you've chosen the right partner, it is always best to do everything in your power to aid and please that person any chance you get instead of waiting for them to do something for you first. Have you ever had an employer shower you with praise, promotions, and raises in pay first, without you first giving it your all? No, it doesn't work that way and never will. You will be out of a job or out of a marriage. Almost without exception, the things that we tend to appreciate and subsequently get the most enjoyment from tend to be the things that were the hardest earned. That holds true with your spouse, job, new boat or car. A child that has earned and saved for a bicycle is inevitably going to take better care of that bike and most likely will get much more enjoyment out of it. The boy that earned, appreciated, and enjoyed that bike, as opposed to the kid who was handed a bike, will likely spend his life practicing the same actions. Why wouldn't he, since it was such a positive experience. In his eyes, that bike is a beautiful thing, he's proud to be seen with it, and at an early age, he is getting a taste for nice things, and he has figured out how to get them. He gets a little older, sees the smart pretty girls, and the not-so-pretty, not-so-smart ones. He's not afraid to put forth a lot of effort to earn the love of the smartest, prettiest girl he sees. In fact, he's used to working for what he gets, so once he lands the girl of dreams, without a thought he knows that the work is not done, in fact it has just begun. He has such an appreciation for this young lady that he knows he'll have to protect that, and continues to work hard to keep her attention. It seems that every time he does something for this girl, she reciprocates twice over. Just like compound interest in a bank account, what seems to start out slowly, quickly snowballs until they never look back.

Most people never learn these lessons or, even more sadly, are never able to experience the pride, appreciation, and enjoyment that started with that little boy's experiences. The majority of marriages or relationships fail because one or both parties never expected to give more than they receive. They want something out of the relationship without putting the effort or work into it first. Many times they never do experience true enjoyment out of the union simply because they don't appreciate what they have. They go into it expecting that it will be perfect first, before they put forth the effort to make it so. How is this any different from expecting an employer to shower you with raises in hopes that you might someday show value?

I'll say it again: You'll never really enjoy anything until you can appreciate it; you'll most likely not learn to appreciate it unless you earned it. I would challenge anyone to come up with any exception.

Many have unknowingly become so used to things just being there for them that they rarely appreciate much of it, and so they don't ever get the full enjoyment out of it. When I say things have just been there, I'm

DON'T FEED THE SQUIRRELS

saying that things have been handed to the people in this country, with a small minority who have sacrificed or worked for it. Subsequently, not having to work for it, no appreciation for it, and you guessed it, not really getting the enjoyment.

Almost anyone reading this is saying, "Ah, not me, I worked for what I've got." Well, think it through. These days we are almost all recipients in some shape or form of government stimulus and intervention. Most jobs are in an industry that benefits from subsidies, tariffs, or handouts. We travel on transportation systems that we didn't pay for. The government didn't even pay for them. Our entire infrastructure, from roads, utilities, police, and military has been provided to us (handout) without compensation. For several decades now it has all been on plastic, on borrowed money. We as a nation and most of us individually have not paid our way, but just like the boy who got the bike handed to him, we continue down the path of receiving, using, discarding, and doing it again.

We've been given an education. Education cannot be forced into your brain, so as a result, two people sit in a class, and one soaks up a lot more than the other. There is an old saying, "You get out of it what you put into it." So, as I said, we are all given an education, some getting more, some less out of it. We've all heard that America is the Land of Opportunity, which is so true, but no different than schooling, you're not likely to get more out of it than you put into it. My dad used to joke, at least I hope he was joking, when I or one of my siblings would mispronounce or say something really stupid, "You can buy 'em books, send 'em to school," and then he would shake his head and say nothing more.

The Land of Opportunity is a gross understatement. A Land of Opportunity, that's what people have traveled across the waters for hundreds of years searching for. Is it coincidental that an overwhelming majority of immigrants who have come here with nothing, from the mass immigrations at Ellis Island to this very day, tend to be the hard working small business owners, working long hours, and building this country, one job at a time? They come here, are given a chance, and coming from where they were, have a great appreciation for what they see here. Just like the young man with the prettiest, smartest girl: it wasn't handed to him, he's earned it and proud of it. You can bet he's going to continue to work hard to keep it.

So, what we can take from this is that every one of our lives are almost, if not entirely the result of decisions made, good or bad, right or wrong, sometimes a single choice or action, and many times a combination of a lifetime of choices. In most cases, the most dramatic negative affects stem simply from a person taking short cuts, the easy way, or not putting enough effort forth; not enough effort into a marriage, education, or career, and it will likely not turn out as well as one would hope. The same goes for nutrition, exercise, caution, or safety. Almost without exception, someone will be standing there asking why someone else has so much more or has it so much better than them without analyzing their own actions and choices.

WHO DESERVES HELP?

I'm sure that there are people who will disagree with me about who deserves to be helped, to what degree, and who has simply gotten what they deserve and will have to live with it. There are no right or wrong answers to these questions. But I'm afraid, that too many times, **help or assistance is doled out according to what is politically popular instead of being based on what is deserved**.

If we come across a man with a cardboard sign saying "Will Work for Beer," should we hand him five bucks? What if the sign reads, "Hungry, Anything Helps?" Should we give the same? More or less? In these cases, most of us are thinking in terms of $5, $10, $20, or maybe even $50. Usually we're just hoping he doesn't make eye contact with us so we can just drive on. Does it matter whether this man, out of no fault of his own, ran across a string of bad luck that put him in this position, or if he is addicted to alcohol or drugs, in which case any money we may give him likely will just go to feed his habit? We've heard that there are a few people who just choose to be homeless and there is nothing you or I can do to help that. It's very likely that this person is in this situation because he made a lot of poor decisions sometime or all through his life. So why should I give him my hard earned money? That's the thinking that goes through our head. I doubt that many of us are thinking, 'Boy, maybe I should take this guy, get him a room and a shower. While I'm at it, feed him, and take him to the doctor for a checkup. I could then take him to the dentist and get those awful teeth fixed up, maybe dentures or whatever it might take.' Of course that may help him and make him feel good today, but then what about tomorrow? I guess I could rent and pay forward indefinitely for a nice apartment in a nice neighborhood and get him out of this bad area. Then of course he's going to continue to get hungry so, you know, I'm not going to be able to come around every day and bring him food, so maybe I should just set it up so he'll receive some coupons for food so he can go to the grocery store and choose what he wants. After all, he might not like what I pick out, he may prefer Lay's potato Chips, and I might have bought him Doritos. In fact, when you think about it, why should he have to get off the couch and go all the way down town to cash his coupons or a check? Maybe I could just send him a card each month loaded with cash that he can use to buy what he chooses. Everybody needs some spending money, so I think I'll make that card so he can draw cash from it to use as he likes. So, now that I've provided him with food, cash, a nice place to live, medical attention and new teeth, I should probably pay a lawyer, maybe put one on retainer to provide any legal services that may come up, whether he might get himself in some kind of criminal trouble, or maybe he just needs to sue somebody or maybe fight a custody battle over one of his illegitimate children. Of course he's got public transportation down the street, and the food bank around the corner...'

I see these guys every day, never know their story, but though I may think that giving him $10 to get some food won't hurt anything, I would never set him up with all the stuff I just listed. If I did that for him, then I would have to wonder about the next guy and the next. I couldn't do that for every one of them, nor would I want to, partly because I don't think they deserve it, but more importantly, I don't think I would really be helping them. We won't do this for the guy on the corner but our government does it every day. And guess what? You never see the people receiving government-issued help out there with a sign that reads "Will Work for Beer" or food or anything else. The fact is you will never see these folks willing to work at all. Why should they? Or, more importantly, how could they when the feeding never seems to stop?

But back to the one guy on the street corner with the cardboard sign, I'll give him 5 or 10 bucks. What about the guy at the convenience store that I was behind one day? I was in a small rural town and stopped to buy a bottle of water. This guy looked to be in his late 20s or near 30ish and had a young girl with him that appeared to be about four or five. He was buying a bunch of junk food, some candy for the girl, a couple of energy drinks and a pack of cigarettes. It seemed like it was taking forever since I was there for business reasons and I had work to do. It was very apparent that this young man was in no hurry to get anywhere, especially not to work. He was negotiating with the clerk, who he seemed to know well, as to how to ring up the energy drinks and cigarettes as real food so it all could be purchased with his EBT card, the State of Washington's version of food stamps. This guy, in my opinion, was a Hoggy Hog, someone who is taking the hand outs, and in this case obviously abusing the system. This young man looked very capable of working. I don't know if his sole income comes from the government, or if he works part time and the government supplements his income. I do know that I was working and I could see no reason why he couldn't be working. If by chance he did work somewhere, part time or even full time, why couldn't he work more? The more likely story is that he had been receiving handouts for so long that this was his typical day: going down to the local store with for free handouts and getting in other people's way. At that moment, the guy was just in the way, in my way and everyone's way. At that moment, at least in my thoughts, that guy was acting like a human being that was just taking up space, contributing nothing. And he apparently had offspring. Was he teaching another generation of Hoggy Hogs how to leach off of others? I'm pretty sure he was going home, meeting up with his Hoggy Hog wife or girlfriend and they were going to have sex and probably spit out some more little Hoggy Hogs, or maybe I should refer to them as Piggy Pigs. Does this guy deserve the free stuff he's getting? No, definitely not. He's buying expensive items that I would not spend my hard earned money on and he's doing it with my hard earned money. No, he is certainly not deserving of overpriced junk food, energy drinks, and cigarettes.

How about the seniors? Most people in this country would agree that we need to and should be able to properly care for our senior citizens. Now just wait a minute. That sounds all great, nice and fuzzy feeling, but what people aren't thinking about and what is happening all too often these days is that the sweet looking old lady may be just an old Welfare recipient. We envision every elderly person as someone who worked hard all their life, paid their taxes, paid into social security and contributed to society. The truth is that we are about to experience the largest group in history entering the senior citizen group and preparing to sit back and be cared for; an alarming percentage of these aging people have spent nearly their entire life living off of the system, and now they are old. Myself, I don't feel any more compelled to continue to give handouts to these aging Hoggy Hogs than I did 10 years or 20 years ago. Except for the fact that it seems to be the politically correct thing to do, why are we so brainwashed to view this particular age group in a different light than non-deserving Hoggy Hogs in their 20s, 30s, or 40s?

There is the old guy that worked a little, played a lot, and spent every paycheck in the bar. He seemed to always get by pretty well and seemed to always have things usually before he could really afford them. He never thought much about the future, and now, what do you know? The future is suddenly here. The guy spent every dime he made, and then some, living it up, buying toys, socializing, always living for the day. He never put away for retirement, didn't want to spend his party money on things like long-term care insurance, or for that matter even basic medical insurance. Now, after 60 years of living a pretty hard life, he's unable to earn a living like he did back when he had a strong back and hands.

Then there is the guy that worked hard all his life, but did everything in his power to avoid paying any taxes, mostly working under the table. He worked just enough each year until he could collect unemployment, ran that out, and then went back to work for a while. He lived his life with no preparation for the future, and he got old, too.

What about the aging woman who worked most of her life waiting tables, sometimes long hours, but when it came to her personal life, she seemed to always make poor decisions. She had 4 or 5 divorces, always moving in with another loser of a man, just to end up each time with restraining orders due to abuse, and each time ending that relationship and then starting again with nothing. Now she finds herself no longer able to carry a drink tray, penniless, and feeling sorry for herself.

These are just a few of the all-too-common scenarios, and in each case, these people who simply lived for today with no thought for tomorrow are there with their hand out expecting to be taken care of. And remember the expected level of care these days is nothing short of what they're being told they should receive, you know, that middle class lifestyle.

One thing that will complicate this issue tremendously in the coming years is not just that these people screwed off for the last thirty years, but now that their sole care is on someone else's shoulders, they could live another 30 years. Do the math; there are simply not enough young people to pay for the old people, especially since at least half of them are contributing nothing. **The math is not difficult people; it simply doesn't work**.

No longer can everything be offered to everyone who expects it, or for that matter, even the ones who've been promised. The only answer for any individual is to immediately turn their life around and begin to be a little more self-reliant, since whatever we've seen in the way of handouts cannot continue.

MORE IS LESS

As our children were growing up, my wife and I constantly juggled work, play, and education. We were busy building a business; Erin would spend time at a co-op daycare where the mothers shared the time in an effort to reduce costs. One thing we were very adamant about was family time. Our concentration was always, **Work Hard, Play Hard**. We couldn't afford long expensive vacations but we took a lot of long weekends. If we weren't camping or fishing, we were riding four wheelers on the dunes, or just getting away to the river or lakes. I would be up late at night loading and preparing for the next day of play. We eventually progressed from the back of the pickup to a motorhome, but when Friday or Saturday morning came we were packed and off. This is a practice that lives on with both my daughter and son today. I'm happy to watch and see that they both work hard and play hard.

One thing that became very evident to me as the years went by is that Erin and I seemed to be doing all the work while the kids were just showing up and having fun. As soon as I realized what was happening, I consciously started paying a little less attention to their stuff when packing. When we would reach our destination, they might be missing something important to them. I found that rarely happened twice, in fact, very quickly, the more responsibility that was left to them, the faster they learned to plan ahead and be a lot more self-reliant.

My son was about sixteen years old, it was summertime; a buddy called and asked him if he wanted to go camping east of the mountains for the weekend. A bunch of his friends were going. About 30 minutes later, a carload of teenagers showed up, music blaring, ready for him to hop in. Matt came out wearing shorts, a tank top, and flip-flops. He had a fishing pole in one hand and a tackle box in the other. He was off and gone, apparently with little thought about anything like a jacket or sweatshirt, maybe a sleeping bag or food. It wasn't till years later that I found out what a miserable, cold, hungry weekend that was for him. He was always in a hurry. There was the time that he and a buddy threw the little Livingston row boat in the back of his truck and took off up the road to go fishing, not taking the time to tie the boat down. Just a short way up the road, the wind caught the boat and it went flying into the air and out onto the road. That could have been disastrous, but thankfully ended with just a big hole in the boat. Then the time he threw the stand-up Jet Ski in the back of his pickup, again not taking the time to tie it down. He got half way down the boat ramp, applied his brakes and the jet ski slid out on the pavement, about 40 feet short of the water, of course in front of a beach full of laughing observers. These were all lessons learned before he was seventeen. Had I continued to take care of everything for him as when he was younger, those lessons would not have been learned until he was much older and the consequences would've undoubtedly been much larger.

I see adult people today who seem to have a rough time even functioning or getting by with what seems to be very few life skills. I've got to think that it may stem from the fact that they always had things done for them and never had to or were able to learn to take care of things on their own.

Today my son juggles business, the equivalent of three jobs, two children, and still seems to be constantly out doing something, whether it's a trip with the family or bass fishing on his own boat. I've seen him on his bass boat, rod in hand, cell phone in his ear, doing business while he is playing. When it comes to the boat, it is always in top shape, of course always tied down, he's always prepared and fully equipped. Dad hasn't been there for a long time, and in fact, he is now Dad to two small children. I trust that before long his kids will be learning those same hard lessons so that they can grow up to be the same capable, self-sufficient individuals as he has become.

The point is that many times by doing less for someone, you're actually doing more.

My daughter's story is very similar. She has been, for as long as I can remember, extremely self-sufficient. She now has three small children, and her young family seems to take the lesson of **Work Hard, Play Hard** to an extreme. It makes me very proud to watch her not do something for her children. Lesson learned. I'm confident that through the years she's experienced and survived enough skinned knees, dented fenders, and near death injuries to not only allow herself to go the rest of her days experiencing life to its fullest, just not quite to a point of being stupid. I see her and her husband shaking their heads at their children's injuries and lessons, just to get out the next day and continue enjoying life.

One example was the time she and a bus load of other seventh graders were coming down the mountain from a ski trip when the brakes went out on the bus and the driver was unable to get the bus back in gear, leaving it to be freewheeling down a steep, narrow, winding mountain road. It was estimated that it had been doing between 85 and 90 mph when it flipped on its side, spinning in circles as it plunged over the steep embankment and eventually landed rear end first in a creek at the bottom of a ravine. She remembers a couple of minutes that must have seemed like eternity, the entire bus load of teenagers without seatbelts being thrown from one side of the bus to the other, to the ceiling and then to the floor, shattered glass and metal against pavement, each millisecond thinking that she may never see her little brother, parents, or friends again. The next day, her picture was on the front page of the Wenatchee newspaper, pictured in a neck brace on a stretcher as the last of the 42 students that were extracted and packed up that mountainside. The youngsters as well as a few adults were rushed to the small local hospital about 3-hours away from all of their families, and then the phone calls began. We didn't receive news until late into the night, and then to hear that our daughter, as well as two of her cousins had been in a horrible bus accident. We started out to make that three-hour drive in about two. You can just imagine the chaos and panic, the tears and smiles as parents of the 42 kids entered that little hospital just about the same time to find that miraculously no one had died and in fact everyone had escaped any really serious injuries. To this day, when Brandi goes up any mountain pass or steep incline she'll clench her fingers and hold on with fear, but it doesn't stop her. She and her family still make the trips, if anything she's now

DON'T FEED THE SQUIRRELS

possibly even more adventurous. I do notice, however, that leading up to any of her own children's field trips at school, she'll ask all the questions and agonize over whether they'll be safe and well supervised, but ultimately, they'll get on that bus and head out, quite often bandaged up from the skinned knee or cut forehead from yesterday's experience.

Watching my kids grow up reminds me of watching birds. It's interesting to watch the birds. The baby birds are high in the nest, opening their beaks when the adult bird shows up with a worm or other food. The baby bird never learns to find food until it leaves the nest. One day the big bird says "**Enough is enough**," and kicks the baby bird out of the nest. It's fly or die birdie, then they are on their own, learning to fly, learning to find food, and learning to not get eaten by predators. Many don't make it, but the ones that do are strong. I see a lot of parents coddle and baby their children far too long, taking care of their every need until one day, they turn 18, and they kick them out of the nest. The kids are doomed for failure, not because they are incapable, but because they're inexperienced and can't figure out why someone isn't there to take care of them. Then, when they do screw up, they can't take responsibility for their mistakes. Had they made some of those mistakes earlier, been allowed to skin their knees a few more times, they would be much better prepared.

Too many children are babied and protected, sheltered and inhibited and then turned out on the streets with a driver's license at 16, able to vote and fight wars at 18, and we wonder why so many can't cut it. Now, our government is encouraging more young adults to stay back in the nest and be on Mommy and Daddy's insurance until the age of 26. You'll notice that the adult birds don't wait until the young birds are bigger than themselves before giving them the boot from the nest. After all, who would they really be helping?

Each day we're seeing hundreds of children coming across the southern borders into this country from Mexico and Central American countries. We hear about it on the news, but the reality is that the majority of them are sixteen or seventeen years old and at ages that we think of as children have been considered adults and forced to act like adults for years in the parts of the world they came from. **It's embarrassing the way so many adults in this country are still being fed and cared for at 19, 20, yes 21, 22, even 28 and 30 years old.** Parents should be ashamed. My dad used to jokingly tell each of us pre-emptively that he was going to break our plate when we turned 18, and we all believed him, in fact not a one of us hung around to find out.

What about when our government takes care of people, giving handouts, getting so many people so dependent on them, and then one day, takes everything away? Again, they could do so much more for people by doing less.

SOME MISTAKES ARE COSTLIER THAN OTHERS

There have been enough studies about the benefits of marriage over the years that certain facts really can't be disputed. Single people are overwhelmingly more likely to live in poverty. Become a single parent and the likelihood exponentially increases. On the other hand, making a marriage commitment for life, and not following through with it tends to be one of the biggest setbacks, both psychological and financial, that most people will suffer in their lifetime. It is said that in the case of divorce that the most you can hope to come out with is half. The reality is, one spouse or the other will fare better, but between lawyers and liquidation costs, there is unlikely to be half left for either party. There is a reason why they refer to it as dissolution, since you're dissolving not only a partnership but two lives.

A married couple can work for years, sometimes a lifetime, building wealth, saving for retirement, and acquiring nice things. Whether you've collectively built up a net worth of $100,000 or $1,000,000, in your mind you're not thinking that you singly are worth half that. The bottom line is your net worth, until one day you end up splitting that and getting what's left after closing costs. Closing costs for a divorce can be expensive, not to mention that for the next two years, both parties are in financial limbo, essentially losing at least two years of earning and saving. There are obviously numerous other reasons that a divorce can be a very negative happening in your life.

So, not being married is not typically a good thing, but getting married and then unmarried is even worse. So, then it seems very clear that getting married and staying that way is by far the preferred option. So why is it that 50-55% of all marriages end before their contractual term is up? Worse yet, the failure rate of a second try is somewhere over 65%. It gets worse; there are less than 30% who are able to make it work the third go around. That's right, third marriages have more than a 70% failure rate.

We've all heard the term "building a life together." Well, have you ever seen a bridge built halfway across a river and stopped? I doubt it. We've read about plenty of bridges or other major projects that have run grossly over budget, ran into unforeseen trouble and complications, or even seemed to turn out to be just one big mistake, but not finishing seemed much worse than just trudging through, as hard as it may have been at the time until it was done. I've spent my career in the building business and I can think of numerous times when that was the case. It could be a single home or an entire community project, but it would become evident early on that this maybe wasn't the absolute best decision in the world. When this happened, I had no choice but to buck up, make the best of it, and get through it. In almost every case, there was some pain, but we stuck with it to the end. Anything short of that would have been so much worse. I've built some things that were not so pretty, some that I was not real proud of, but still followed it through to the end. Some were just not a good idea from the start, you know, another bad decision.

Had I quit and bailed out of any one of those tough projects, there would have been no one there to bail me out, no one to make me whole; I'd have just been broke. And why should anyone be there to support me after that, since it wouldn't have even been that I couldn't finish it but that I didn't finish it.

So, more than half the people who are in the middle of building a life together make the decision to halt the project before completion. For many, this is not the first or even the second project they've bailed on, each time splitting up the pie until there is really no wonder they end up in poverty. And in many cases, it wasn't that they couldn't finish up, it's that they didn't.

It would be crazy to claim that there is never a reason to end a marriage before the end of its term. Rarely will either party take responsibility or blame; instead they will point the finger at the other party. The truth is that there is almost always plenty of blame to go around.

I'm not here to cast blame or even judge, I am simply pointing out one of the common reasons why people end up either in poverty or at the very least in need of a hand out now or later in life. I'm saying that I don't feel that I should have to pay to support someone who put themself in that position willingly.

The problem gets overwhelmingly worse when there are children involved. In many ways, our government is again responsible for creating this safety net that can look more appealing, and certainly easier than sticking it out. For the divorced single mother, she is pretty much assured that someone will be there to provide her and her children with housing, food, and medical services for what appears to be an indefinite length of time. For the ex-husband of that divorced mother (who is now receiving government benefits), there is little hope of getting his head above water. Between child support for children he may seldom see, and many times repayment for the welfare handed out, he is lucky if he can keep a roof over his head.

Children or not, at the very least, at the onset of a breakup, a couple suddenly goes from paying for one household to two. As we've seen, a household today is not the household of the 50s or 60s. There are plenty of reasons why it has typically gone to a two income household, and that's everything from higher rents, bigger homes, to cable and internet bills. It costs about the same to cook for two as it does one, so break it up and the food costs nearly double. Two households to heat or cool, you name it; you've pretty much doubled your monthly overhead, coupled with the fact that you need to purchase a second couch, blender, knives, and forks.

It gets worse in that suddenly the split couple will find themselves single and free, which means that they'll no longer be spending their evenings watching television and eating popcorn. No, two people going out, doing most anything social-related will cost a tremendous amount more than the old routine. If they do have children, there will be more need for babysitting services, daycare, you name it.

Sometimes one single event, like a divorce, can pretty much assure that both parties will spend the rest of their lives financially devastated, and very likely dependent upon the system, and as long as there are so many safety nets out to assist these poor people who willingly, knowingly put themselves in this position, the less effort people will put into making things work and sticking together.

Again, why should I pay for these people who give up, who throw in the towel sometimes simply because they want a more exciting life? There is really no coincidence that over half the marriages break up and that more than half the people in the country are living in or near poverty.

To sum it up, you can't afford to be single but you really can't afford to be married and then single.

I was sitting at a poker table when someone calling a hand on the river referred to his action as "good money after bad." I responded by saying something like, "I don't understand. I'm not sure that I've ever seen bad money." A young man, maybe in his early thirties, immediately spoke up as if he really knew what he was talking about and said, "Good money after bad is the money spent on your first marriage." He then went on to say, "The good part of the good money after bad is the money spent to get out of the trouble from the bad money already spent."

Marriage is just one huge example of how each of our decisions, large or small, right or wrong, good or bad dictate the quality of our lives and futures, and more importantly, our ability to be a contributing citizen as opposed to a Hoggy Hog. If you can abandon that bridge mid-span without it affecting me and the few people left in this nation paying the debts of others, then OK, but don't come crying when the feeding trough is no longer full.

DON'T FEED THE SQUIRRELS

CEO IS NOT A FOUR-LETTER WORD

We've all heard of the person who started in the mail room or at the bottom of the company and is now running the company. There are the people who get a job, work 30 years with little advancement, the ones who move up in the ranks, and everything in between. Over the years, I've employed or interviewed people who spent their entire adult life moving from one job to another, sometimes from one occupation to another, and never spent more than two-years in one place. Some did this by choice, in a constant effort to better themselves, and others just could never last at any one place.

I've often noticed that just about anyone can scam their way along through a job for a period of time, usually about two years, before their true worth or lack of worth surfaces. Many times they self-sabotage themselves because things are getting difficult, and it is essentially easier for them just to move on rather than learn to adapt to their surroundings.

So, assuming each person was working a full-time job, 2080 hours a year, why is one person content with earning $10 an hour or $20,800 a year, while another earns $20 an hour for an annual income of $41,600 per year? This same comparison can be made to the person earning $80,000 or $100,000 a year. Each person gets up each morning, commutes to and from their job, and between the 8 hours of work and the commute, they arrive back home about 9-1/2 hours later, having used up nearly 60% of their awake hours of that day. They do that approximately 71% of the days each week. They each buy the same gasoline, suffer similar wear and tear on their vehicle, but one is content to continue day after day, week after week, many times for a lifetime to earn a fraction of what another may earn.

Generally the stark differences in compensation vary as to the type of work performed, the skills required, or the education or degrees needed. The person waiting tables may not earn as much as the plumber, and the plumber not as much as the accountant, and so on. But no different than most things in life, whether it be the price of beef, a home, or the wages paid for a particular task or service, it almost always comes down to supply and demand. Any economics expert can tell you that the government can mess with things and change them to a certain degree and for a certain length of time, but basic economics always come down to supply and demand. From time to time, our society will put out an overabundance of lawyers, or a shortage of doctors, and respectively the earnings of the people in those occupations will elevate or decline accordingly.

Typically, the higher paying occupations are those requiring a specific degree, thereby limiting the number of people available to fill those positions. There are far fewer doctors, those who made significant sacrifices and efforts to get where they are, than there are assembly line laborers or fry cooks who just had to show up, and offer up their 8 hours. For the most part, an entry level or minimum wage position could be filled at a moment's notice with most anyone off the street, whereas the doctor, lawyer, or engineer's position draws from a much smaller pool of candidates. Furthermore, if a law firm is able to bill out at rates of several hundreds of dollars per hour, there's certainly more room to pay the individual lawyer at a much higher rate than can the restaurant owner who is trying to stay in business selling a breakfast plate for $7.99.

But this is America, the land of the free (free stuff). There is not a citizen in this nation who is bound by slavery or servitude, with the exception of course of any illegal activities. Each person is free from the time they are in their teens until the day they die to choose how and where to spend their time. They can choose a particular job or occupation, work at it for any length of time, decide it's not for them, and walk away and try something different. Many people will find a job that maybe isn't their dream job or occupation, and work at it while they're looking for something better, or possibly while they're going to school to better prepare themselves for a different or better career opportunity.

For hundreds of years people have traveled across oceans to other lands, such as the United States, for the opportunities to get work and a paycheck, learn a trade, and better themselves. Often they came here with nothing but what was on their back, leaving everything behind. But more recently, all we seem to hear about is the lack of job mobility or the difficulty for people to travel or relocate for employment. Plain and simple, a person living in the poverty-stricken inner city or a backwoods isolated little town may be better off getting out of town and going where they are needed. It comes down to supply and demand, again. If there are 50 working-age people in the little town and only 10 jobs, someone needs to look elsewhere. School kids have had to learn that lesson. If they attend a large high school with a large enrollment and wish to play basketball, it will undoubtedly be much harder competing to make the team than the person from the small town with fewer kids to choose from. Each team is still only going to play 5 on the court and roster maybe 15. And very similar to business, the coach of that large school is much more likely to have a better team due to the fact that he has a larger field to choose from. This is supply and demand learned at an early age. And what's the chance that a kid walks onto the court, with no experience, practice or skills, and makes the team? The kid that never picked up a ball and goes to try outs expecting to just offer up his body and time will assuredly be disappointed. The sad thing is that many never learn the lesson; they'll go out into the world, offering up their body and time, expecting that the employer will pay them for showing up. If they are lucky enough to land that minimum wage starting position, it will only be because most or all the other people before him made themselves more valuable, moved up or out, and opened the position for the less desirable. Sadly, there may either be too many unskilled bodies like him or not enough entry-level jobs where the employer is able to pay an unskilled worker minimum wage. After all, that restaurant owner is still only able to charge $7.99 for that breakfast plate. So, why can't the restaurant owner simply charge more for the meal and pay employees more? Well, that might work if there were more people in the community that were working at better jobs with better skills and higher pay. The fact is that far too many people have not put much effort into bringing value to themselves. **They just want to walk on and play. Well, sorry guys, society doesn't need that many bench warmers.** Supply and demand, you know.

Just like each worker has to commute to work, they each have to pay for food, shelter, and the basic needs for themselves and their family. Let's just say that for the low-wage earner, it takes every dime they make just to get by. That would mean that if they could earn $2 an hour more, times 2080 hours a year, they would have $4,160 additional dollars for extras. I'm assuming no taxes because typically the lower wage earners are paying little or no taxes. They had nothing left over after their basic needs, now they have four thousand bucks. The point is that we all have the costs of just getting by, but each cent after that is gravy, it's the cream, and it's the difference. And once that person finds a way to make themselves more valuable and not just get by, but to get ahead, four thousand bucks ahead, wouldn't it be natural to want to go the next step, and earn that next four thousand bucks, that next $2 per hour? One might think that the sky's the limit, so why not just keep moving up and making more, and so on. You may think, 'Hah, it's not just about money.' But frankly, yes it is, at least until you've provided for your basic needs and earned enough to not only provide an enjoyable life for you and your family but to assure that you won't be a drag on society. **Everyone has a moral obligation to properly provide for themselves as well as the people they bring into this world.**

President Obama has repeatedly tried every which way to prove some good in the Obama Care law. He came out with, "People will now have the choice not to work if they so choose," like that's a good thing. One of the reasons people may have continued to work at a particular job was the added benefit of the employer-paid health care insurance. Now that the government, society, the tax payers, well no, the rich (the only ones really paying taxes) have promised to provide all the health care coverage to the people who "choose" not to work, don't you think that there will be many more people who will choose not to work? Well, I guess that whittles away at that supply and demand thing. If enough people choose not to work, I guess it will make a little less competition for those entry level jobs, maybe even to a point that the bench warmer may be brought off the bench. Good luck on getting your eggs over easy, or the drain plug tightened at the quickie lube.

At some point, after a person takes care of their own personal obligations, and at the very least becomes a self-sufficient citizen of society, and assures that their offspring have the knowledge and lessons to do the same, then and only then, they should enjoy the right to pursue happiness. It would be nice if everyone just loved going to work each day, looked forward to arriving early and staying late, but frankly, that's just not the case. There are a lot of jobs that just don't go along with that. I once worked a temporary job at a mill on what was called "the chain." The job consisted of standing in a 10' area taking boards off of a chain-driven conveyor and stacking them on pallets and in bins. The minutes seemed like hours, and the hours like days. There must have been someone watching from afar and turning the speed up and down because it seemed like the faster I worked, the faster it came down the line. I worked there for three weeks, found something better, and moved on. So, if someone is working at a job that they hate, well, good for them – for a while. They have a moral obligation to provide for themselves as well as to be a contributing member of society. After that, if they stay at the job they hate, well that's their own fault.

I heard it said on a radio program **"The people complaining about how much the CEOs are making are the parents who didn't teach their kids how to be CEO."** The fact is that, as people are griping about the enormous incomes of a few, what they are really unhappy about is their own income. It's a lot like that ill-prepared kid walking onto the basketball court and complaining about Michael Jordon making too much. Supply and demand, people. There are far too many people not willing to put forth the effort, but more than willing to ridicule the successful. Yet the people qualified to run that large corporation are few. I know someone who is a commercial fisherman, and also someone who is a potato farmer. Both fish as well as potatoes vary greatly in terms of the price they will bring from year to year, depending on the amount of fish or potatoes caught or grown, and the demand at the time. Neither of them can control the demand or the amount of product their competitors may be bringing to market. They can, however, control the type or quality of product they bring to market. They can choose from year to year to fish for a different variety of fish, or plant a product that may be more in demand. I continue to hear, "There are not enough good jobs." The self-employed, or the entrepreneurial people don't complain, they look around and figure it out.

People, be aware and teach your kids: **THE JOBS ARE NOT GOING TO MAKE THEMSELVES FOR YOU, YOU HAVE TO MAKE YOURSELVES FOR THE JOBS.**

The self-employed or entrepreneurial, the job makers, have never been given "extended benefits." They have never been paid while being retrained. They've never been handed Hoody's; they've had to make sure there were enough nuts put away for the winter. Then they had to protect those nuts so the Hoggy Hogs didn't come along and take them, or worse, from being redistributed by the government. The job creators don't always find the opportunities in their back yard, they sometimes have to travel.

We were recently riding in a shuttle van from an Arizona airport to our vacation home and talking to the driver. He had been living in Arizona for a few years but originally came from Africa. He was working as a shuttle van driver, which is a piece work position meaning the more he worked or the smarter or more efficiently he worked, the more money he could make. He explained that while working this job, he had been preparing to take a test to be certified to drive big rig trucks. He had a job lined up in Texas where three of his cousins, all from Africa, were presently working. He was assured by his cousins that immediately upon getting his license and getting to Texas, if he worked long hours as they were doing, he would be earning in excess of $120,000 a year. Just as his cousins were doing, he would work three weeks at a time and return for a week to Arizona, where his wife would remain, working her own job. This reminded me of my younger days during the 1980–1981 recession when there seemed to be no construction work. I was given an opportunity to work in another part of the state that was too far for a daily commute, so I would leave early Monday morning and return late Friday evening, coming back home to my wife and young daughter. I brought a borrowed camper to stay in during the week on the job site. Some of the other workers and I cooked and ate around a campfire and lived pretty inexpensively throughout the week. I hated being away from home, but I was able to work long hours and make pretty good money while the majority of people in the trades were out of work.

Today I'm hearing and reading about the work available, both in North Dakota and Texas, for just about anyone willing to show up and work hard. These jobs pay well and are available for people without a lot of special skills, but who are willing to put forth some effort. Between the oil fields and refinery work, there are areas in those states where the jobs are seriously out-pacing the places for the workers to live or stay. So, at a time with nearly record unemployment, how can anyone in one of the 50 states claim that they can't find work? Even more disturbing is why any extended unemployment compensation checks could be sent out until each one of these job positions have been filled. It seems like a common happening when we see people who have emigrated here from other countries taking advantage of the opportunities available to them as the rest of the American people sit on their butts complaining that their government check isn't enough or that the benefits are running out after two years.

Over and over you'll see a person collecting benefits for two years, claiming they can't find work just to miraculously find a job two weeks after their extended benefits run out. Are these people stupid, lazy, or were the handouts just too easy to get and too tempting to turn down?

When the 2008 financial meltdown set in, housing construction pretty much came to a halt, putting the majority of people in the home building trades out of work. Through some foresight or just plain dumb luck, my family and I were in a position where we could continue building and even step it up from what we had been doing during the crazy boom times. We had resisted leveraging ourselves like most of our competitors, so when almost all building lots and projects were going back to the banks, we were (for the most part) the only ones there to purchase them. Again, supply and demand; a short time earlier there may have been hundreds of builders lined up to purchase home sites and properties, but now there were almost none. And as you would expect due to supply and demand, there being virtually no competition, those lots and plats were able to be purchased at a much lower price. My brother jokingly compared our situation or opportunity to being like Forrest Gump when his was the only shrimp boat to have survived the storm, which meant not only more shrimp for him but the price of shrimp was very favorable to him. So, as we purchased building lots at a fraction of what the going rate may have been a year earlier, we were able to build homes, mark them up a reasonable amount, and still sell them at a much lower price than anything else on the market. This was not only good for us, but was somewhat of a lifesaver for most of our suppliers and subcontractors, since there was simply no one else building for quite a few years. Though we had typically employed 40–50 direct employees, the majority of our other work was contracted out to subcontractors, most of them being small guys with a few employees. Just prior to the economic downturn we were surrounded by every type of subcontractor and supplier, from heating and siding contractors to lumber wholesalers and roofers, all of them with plenty of business to keep them busy. In what seemed like overnight, that all changed, and as you would expect, due to supply and demand the prices of materials as well as services and labor plummeted. Although I feel for the individuals that were suddenly forced to earn much less than they previously had, like any surviving business, we were able to build our product for much less, allowing us to pass those savings on to the home buyer. Again, an example of supply and demand: we were able to employ the best of the best in all the trades. Anyone who wasn't very good at what they did, and sadly a lot of people who were, left the industry. Many got completely out of the trades, not to return. And, of course, a few short years later, when housing began to recover and as soon as the need for plumbers, siders, and finish carpenters grew around mid-2013 to 2014, there was quickly a shortage of skilled craftsmen and, you guessed it, due to supply and demand, prices skyrocketed and availability became problematic. The subcontractors who had been doing our work while most of the others were out of work had the majority of the best workers, and as soon as the other guys had a few jobs lined up they were out hiring those skilled workers , paying whatever they needed to lure them away. And so the cycle goes, it's happened before and it will assuredly happen again.

DON'T FEED THE SQUIRRELS

BORN-AMERICAN AMERICANS

These days it seems that there is no way to describe the different ethnic groups or nationalities without someone finding fault or taking offense. In the residential home building industry, the worksite has grown much more diversified over the years. For instance, 25 years ago you would see almost exclusively white male workers. Today, the Caucasian worker is, without a doubt, the minority. If you speak of the Russian workers, someone gets angry, correcting you to say that they are Ukrainian; Hispanic or Mexican may be the preferred reference to one person and offensive to another, even though just about everyone else refers to anybody who is Norwegian, Irish, or Italian as "the white guy."

With some exceptions, when describing the worker today, we can almost break people down into two categories, the "born-American American" and the "came-to-America American." Take, for instance, the van driver who came from Africa or all of his cousins, are they Americans? Have they become citizens of America, are they in the process of applying and becoming American citizens? I don't know. At what point do they become Americans? After they've been here how long? And, even more importantly, how much do they have to contribute and participate in our economy and society before they become or we can or should consider them Americans? I think you'll find there is a large division between people who want to boot them all out and the people who value their contributions and welcome them here. Probably the biggest factor as to how they are and will continue to be accepted is whether they arrived here legally or not, so much so that there exists constant debate and conflict over whether some of those here illegally should be granted amnesty, or if they should not be allowed to stay unless or until they've gone through the same painstaking process that a lot of other Americans have performed when immigrating to this country. The one thing that so many Americans forget when it comes to this issue is that America has always been made of people from other places, all races and nationalities, and for the most part nearly all of us are descendants of ancestors who came here from other countries. For hundreds of years, most of the fighting and hatred has stemmed from the fear that someone from the outside was here taking "our" jobs. It may have been the Swedes fighting the Irish, or anyone who had been here for anytime at all, looking down on the Chinese, always afraid that someone else was taking or going to take their work. Today, it seems that is not so much the case. It seems as if the people coming to America are filling the jobs that the born-American Americans don't want to do, or aren't very good at doing.

More and more, it seems that the dirty jobs, the not-so-prestigious jobs, are overwhelmingly being performed by the came-to-America

Americans. Fifteen years ago, I would travel to areas such as Las Vegas or Phoenix where there was a lot of residential building going on, studying and looking at the construction and marketing methods being practiced, as well as the products being offered, in a constant quest to better compete and keep ahead of the competition in my home state. It was obvious that the vast majority of the trades were being performed by Mexican or Hispanic workers. Fast forward to today, and in the state of Washington, if you walk onto most any jobsite, you'll pretty much hear 90% Mexican or Russian style music. Asian or Black workers are a rarity, at least in the residential industry. There are still a number of the old white guys who work as skilled carpenters, etc., but a dwindling number of young white, American-born men or women are coming up in the trades.

A lot of the compensation is piecework or compensated relative to the amount of work completed. As a result, a worker has to work hard and fast. As a general rule, the came-to-America American worker is not afraid to work hard and long, and could it be that they are stronger and more resilient, because they seem to rarely get hurt. I hate to profile and certainly don't want to imply that every born-America American worker is lazy and weak, as many are not, but these guys come on the job, fake injuries, and sit home collecting compensation for months, and in many cases, years. An employer is very limited in the questions they may ask when interviewing a potential employee and, at least in the state of Washington, they have to make a conditional offer of employment before they can ask the important questions, most of which are directly related to "can you perform the job?" So, OK, we can't discriminate or deny employment for a number of valid reasons, but come on, would you want to hire an overweight, out of shape, weak-looking smoker that has a hard time breathing just sitting in the interview chair when the job will entail lifting, bending, and maybe even climbing a ladder or a flight of stairs? I know the tattoos up both arms and his neck, and all the face hardware may not directly relate to whether he can function out on the jobsite, but to an old guy like me, as many employers are, it certainly paints a picture as to the priorities in this guy's life and the types of decisions he makes. How about the fact that his work history has holes in it, long, unexplained periods of time when he wasn't working? And what about dressing for the job you want? What if a guy walks into my office looking like some kind of Yuppie prep boy with soft manicured hands, when what I want to see is a guy come in with his work boots, like he's at least seen or done some construction-related work; 9 times out of 10 this type of guy proceeds to tell me how much money he needs to get by. He'll tell me about all of his payments and child support, which, me being who I am, the employer, makes me think about the life choices this guy makes. If I let him talk long enough, before I escort him to the door and tell him, "We'll let you know," then I'll hear about all the bum raps he's gotten and the rotten bosses he's had in the past. He'll tell me about each of the other builders he's worked for and how poorly managed their business was. This is not an anomaly. This is how the typical interview goes with the typical born-American American worker. I can't say how many times I've walked out of my office shaking my head, bewildered as to how guys like I've just described could possibly think that I would actually want to give them a paycheck, and I feel angry that they've wasted my time. I have quite often made the comment to someone in the office after the guy left, that it seems like some people are actually trying not to get hired.

The came-to-America American comes in looking for work. He is in a hurry because he probably had to take an hour off from the job he was working that day. He's in his work clothes, driving his work truck outfitted with tools, and he is ready to work. There is no mention of how much "he needs" to get by. He doesn't tell me what he could do, he tells me what he has been doing, and maybe he's very busy but looking for something better or better pay. Now, that's the kind of guy that I want to pay and am willing to pay.

These guys know how to go out and get a job, and they will rarely be out of work for long. Have the majority of the born-American Americans forgotten how to get a job, and as a result, they're not able to do a job? Are they that clueless as to what it means to offer a day's work for a day's pay?

Quite often I stop at the 7-11 convenience store in the morning, or at the local truck stop gas station to grab a cup of coffee for the road. That's where you'll see the working guys and work trucks. I notice these things because over the years I've had a similar practice when considering going into a different or unknown market or purchasing a housing project in an out-of-the-way area, one that I'm not familiar with. I have gone up to a small town and just parked along the road with a cup of coffee and watched the vehicles passing. Starting from about 6:00 a.m. until about 9:00 a.m., the demographics of the people as well as the vehicles change dramatically. I've done this a number of times in an attempt to get a gut feeling of the type of people that are living in the area, the people that we will be trying to sell homes to. That's what the small builder or small businessman does, where the corporate office builder, say the national builder will be looking at that market as if it is the same as a project 30 miles away, when in reality, the product that should be brought to market may be something for an entirely different demographic, whether that be related to ethnic or economic differences. Taking time to scout a new location gives me an idea if the potential homebuyer needs a two-car garage for the BMW or if the pick-up guy is going to need or be looking for a third bay or maybe room on the side of the house to park his drift boat. One thing that is easily distinguishable during the early hours at the convenience store is the came-to-America Americans from the born-American Americans. From the insulation installers, to the roofers, the big trucks that say "Clean Your Crawlspace," or most any other dirty, difficult job you can think of, it will be filled by the came-to-America guys, not the born-here guys. They sell a lot of tacos and taquitos early in the morning, and it isn't until much later that the Hoggy Hog young women come strolling in, dressed in pajamas and slippers, using an EBT card to buy junk food and a pack of smokes.

Over the years I have retained great admiration for the working guy, the one that isn't afraid to get dirty. Maybe it's because back in the day, I did most of those jobs myself, and some of those jobs were so dirty and unpleasant that I worked hard to bring myself up the ladder to where I no longer had to perform those tasks, but can still appreciate the ones that do.

I, in no way, want to imply that we don't have very hard-working, intelligent young people who are not too good to do those dirty jobs, because I've seen close-up some of the best. But I can say that they are few and far between. We've all heard it said that, "The young people these days just don't want to work." I don't completely agree with that and don't want to believe that. I can tell you that, at least in the blue collar jobs I've been referring to, there aren't a lot of mentors around to take these young people by the hand and train them. I have seen firsthand a select few young people come up from an entry-level position, and advance very quickly to becoming their own bosses, owning their own companies, and doing very well. These stand-out individuals took it upon themselves to tag along with others, many times on their own time, in order to learn a specific trade. They got good at their job, worked long hours, saved their money, and well, you know the story. It doesn't matter the field of work; it could be the home builder, the barista or the person painting fingernails, the ambitious, entrepreneurial person still has a tremendous opportunity here in this nation. As a matter of fact, it seems that as a larger percentage of people don't put forth the effort to better themselves, the wider the window becomes for the few energetic smart ones. This is another example of supply and demand.

So, I want to say that the American Dream is still alive, still available, but unfortunately, the came-to-America Americans seem to be the ones that are predominantly earning and living it. They are in overwhelming numbers living the dream, while a large share of the born-American Americans are whining, griping, and not reaching for the brass ring. These other individuals are proving that the dream is still there for the taking. The problem again stems from all the handouts. **The born-American Americans have been filling up on Hoody's for so long, they don't want or know how to feed themselves.**

DON'T FEED THE SQUIRRELS

PASS ON THAT LESSON

There was a recent article about a third-grade girl who got on the bus in the morning and went to school, spent the entire day in class, and only at the end of the day when she was to get back on a bus to go home was it discovered that not only had she taken the wrong bus that morning, she had gone to the wrong school and attended the wrong class. My daughter, who is a teacher, then told me a similar story about a teacher she knows who pulled his child out of a school after his experience. Apparently his child had been home ill for an entire week and when the father went to school to get the student's work from the teacher, he was told of how well his son had been doing all week and found that the teacher was completely unaware that the child had not been in his seat all week.

Sadly, it's not only in the classroom where attention is not being paid to the teachings and what is being taught to our children. Throughout school and into our adult lives, many, if not most of us are slipping between the cracks and either not being taught, but what's worse is that in many cases we're being taught the wrong lessons.

There is simply not a thing in this world that could not be greatly improved with education or better education. The lessons are out there to be had, but a person has to either be very observant, or very lucky to get it right and soak it in. Our government, the media, and now social media have had both a devastating as well as positive impact on people's lives.

We believe what we hear. We're constantly hearing that the answer is better access to higher education, at the same time we see evidence that the majority of high school graduates entering college are nowhere close to being prepared, either academically or socially. Though I can't think of an argument against more young people getting a college experience as well as a degree, I think more importantly we are writing off the rest of the younger generation. What is far more important is assuring that all children get a decent basic education. For so long now, we as a country have been failing drastically in early education.

Back in the post-World War II era, television was relatively new and was replacing radio; it was as popular and exciting to people, as the Internet is today. It was also an era when Hollywood movies featured movie stars smoking cigarettes. The most common commercials showed cigarettes and the people who smoked them as glamorous and cool, so much so that one of the popular brands was even named Kool, with a "K." Boy, now there's a subliminal message. Subsequently, for decades following, lung cancer proved to be the number one killer in America. It seemed that everyone's parents and grandparents smoked. I know mine

DON'T FEED THE SQUIRRELS

did, and as a result every one of my relatives died an early agonizing death.

Then in 1964, the Surgeon General's report came out linking smoking to lung cancer and the government began to restrict tobacco companies' advertising, and required educational notices on cigarette packs. Sixty years ago, we really could better depend on our government to make some good moves. As a result of those actions, in conjunction with continuously adding heavy taxes to tobacco products, by 2012, the percentage of Americans smoking had dropped from 42 percent to around 12 percent. Was it this scare tactic type of education, the restricting of glorified advertising, or simply the economic taxation that was responsible for one of the greatest public-health successes since the battle against polio? One thing that's certain is that there's probably not a person in our nation today that is unaware of the risks involved in smoking. At the same time the number of adults globally who smoke has increased to nearly a billion. While we've seen miraculous reductions in the United States, as well as most of the other developed nations that have warned and educated their people, the poorer developing nations have seen tobacco use skyrocket. Coincidentally, at the same time those same nations have seen an increase in marketing by tobacco companies. Could the drastic increase in smoking in these poorer countries be directly related to marketing that shows how cool or "Kool" smoking can be? Or is it more directly due to the people of those nations finally getting a few bucks in their pockets? Maybe a little of both, but isn't it sad that the poorest people in the world finally get a buck or two in their pockets and the spreaders of this cancer are there to take it from them?

Education has worked in the U.S. to the point where approximately 20% of men now smoke, as opposed to about 55% of

Chinese men. It's a horrible thought, but could this be part of their plan? We've all heard "China is going to own us," mostly referring to the U.S. debt that they own. It's common knowledge in the insurance actuary world that one of the cheapest illnesses for customers to get is lung cancer. It's not because it doesn't cost a lot to treat, but because a person with lung cancer is treated for a short time and dies. Done deal, no more benefits, that's one policy holder they will not have to keep alive into their expensive aging years. But the Chinese, on the hand, not only don't have the burden of Obama Care to support, they will continue to have their population stay around through their productive years and about the time they are about to become a real liability they'll die off, thereby putting them ahead of the United States yet again, at least financially.

Another example of how educating our people can make a drastic difference is when it comes to the reduction of teen pregnancy. The 1960s were just the start of "Free Love" and the perception that if a person was not having sex with multiple partners and at younger and younger ages, there must be something wrong with them. Television and movies have continued to get more and more provocative and graphic when it comes to young people and sex. I think even the most open-minded of us would agree that the media has been spreading a very dangerous message to our young people. But as widespread and common as it is to see teens and young adults participating and enjoying seemingly unlimited sex, and the pressures that some of these young adults are subjected to, nothing seems as powerful as a message geared toward fear and consequences. This type of message has been effective in the U.S., as teen pregnancies have been greatly reduced in recent years. There have been a couple of popular TV Shows, like *16 and Pregnant*, and *Teen Mother* that a lot of that reduction has been attributed to. Again, this downturn is very likely due to the fear factor, but the truth is, maybe just a little education provided to these young people, both girls and boys, has given them a little better direction and made them realize that there may be no one out there to look after them except themselves. Of course there is always the financial side of the argument, and a significant reduction in babies born to unwed mothers was correlated with Welfare Reform legislation. After all, there was a time that our system and handouts almost encouraged and compensated young girls and women to have more babies out of wedlock. It's not to say that young people today are refraining from sexual activity, in fact they are probably even more sexually active, but thanks to education, both from in-school education programs as well as popular shows on television showing the down side to risky behavior and unprotected sex, less people are ruining their lives or becoming lifetime recipients of public assistance.

One obvious tool that is at our fingertips today is social media, which young people love and understand so well. How this technology pans out in terms of its educational use is yet to be seen, but the opportunities are unlimited.

But what about the parents? It seems that in this busy world, parents just expect that they can send their kids off to school and it is someone else's responsibility to teach their child everything they need to know. Well, not only have we seen that it's just not going to happen; it simply should not be expected. There is one person who is solely responsible for the education of a child and that is the parent, and in the event that there are two parents in the equation, it's even better, but that doesn't let one of them off the hook. The problem is that as much as none of us want to admit it, even to ourselves, most of us are not fit to teach. Nearly all of us have been doing a really poor job of running our own lives while our children have been watching. Is there a reason why we should expect that they would watch us screw up our lives and then do things differently?

One of the easiest teachings any parent can instill in their children is to stop giving their kids everything. Just stop it. These habits of access to instant gratification are hard to break. It's like a drug, and one that is hard to get off of. Most parents wouldn't put heroin out with their child's daily vitamins, but in many ways, the habits you're getting your kids hooked on are equally as bad and possibly tougher to kick, especially when they won't even know or believe that they have a problem. By allowing kids to have things without working for them, or not holding them responsible for things, you are feeding that habit and appetite for instant gratification. It's a drug. They watch you buying that new car with the promise of paying for it later, they watch you go to the mall and use that plastic card to get things you don't need before you can afford them. You may as well be sitting in your living room with a syringe and needle stuck in your arm. Most of the poor decisions, the ones you wish they wouldn't make stem from the desire for instant gratification, and they are modeling their behavior on what they've seen from their parents.

If parents, not just the "other ones," but us too, would just show the same example of what we hope our children will follow, that's the best education they can get.

How do you, or will you feel when you hear your teen or young adult child carrying on with every fourth or fifth word being the "F" word, or some other cuss word that doesn't really belong in an intelligent person's conversation? Is this a result of your teaching? How does that make you feel? It's not too late to fix it. I've got a friend that was in his mid-fifties, when he one day committed to stop drinking and cussing. He has from time to time fallen off the wagon when it comes to the cussing but today he is a much better man. And my guess is that his children have learned from him, too, both before and after the transformation.

We've all seen the stark difference between the "Larry the Cable Guy" type and the more articulate individual who seems to know a little something about everything, can feel comfortable in most any social situation, and is able to hold his or her own in any conversation. Now look at your child, which is he leaning towards? Is he spending far too much of his time playing video games or is he out there mingling and learning to communicate with others? Where does he learn his behaviors? Is it from Dad, who spends his time on the couch watching sports and can recite any sport statistic but couldn't tell you a thing about the issues in the upcoming election? Maybe the lessons come from Mom, who can tell you the winners and losers from the last three series of Dancing with the Stars, all the happenings of the Kardashians, and is enjoying the good life she's been living, but has no idea that it may be about to come to an end since she hasn't turned on the news or picked up a newspaper in some time. Parents, you can't just wait and see how your child's life turns out, the lessons are learned now and, sorry, but like it or not, you are the teacher.

Once your child goes out into the working world and gets a few paychecks, lives on his own and makes a life for himself, when he comes home to visit, you probably hope he doesn't drive up in an old clunker of a car blowing blue smoke and dragging the muffler, but what if he drives up in a new jacked-up pickup or brand new Camaro, grinning from ear to ear? In talking to him, he tells you that the payments are only $500 per month for the next 84 months (that's 7 years), are you going to be happy and proud of him, or will you shake your head in worry and disappointment? Where do you suppose the kid learned how to do that?

As my children were growing up, whether at the dinner table or in general discussion around the house, they were not allowed to use the word "sue" as in the legal term. If some related conversation would arise, we could say something like "take legal action," but I just didn't like the term "sue" or "I'll sue you," because it seemed that I heard the term far too often, from children to adults, threatening to sue someone for the silliest of things. Back then, and even more so now, it seems that very few people are willing to take responsibility for themselves and their actions, or even sometimes things that just happen. It seems that any time something negative happens to someone, they have to find someone to blame, someone else to be responsible for it. I think I may have learned this from my parents because I remember they would often speak negatively about anyone suing someone. Parents nowadays blame the teacher when a student fails, we blame the banks when they loaned us 100% on our home and the value happens to go down, and we continue to send this message of not taking responsibility to our children. Maybe the next time the child leaves his bike out and it gets ran over or stolen, or he leaves his coat on the playground, he should go without a bike or coat until he can earn another one. The squirrels won't even bother to hide or stash the Hoody's if they just expect that they'll keep coming. Envision your child at thirty years old. How do want them to act? I think we would all like them to turn out better than us. And if they don't, whose fault is it? Now don't tell me you can blame that on someone else, too.

We're always going to love our kids. For the most part, we'll be proud of them even if the rest of the world doesn't see them through the same eyes. But from an aesthetic standpoint, we can't expect that our children will all look like the actors and actresses we see every day on the screen or in the tabloids, since let's face it, a certain amount of it depends on genetics, so they're going to look at least to some degree, like us. But will they look like us the way we are, or the way we could have been or should have been? Let's face it, there are very few of us who, by the time we've reached middle age, haven't let ourselves go maybe just a little. Most of us go through a period where we feel like we're doing pretty good and then one day we wake up, look in the mirror, and wonder how we packed on those extra pounds, or notice that the weight distribution just doesn't seem to go where it did a few years ago. We know what's causing that, and we know what to do about it. We sometimes even will get back on the band wagon and aggressively start taking better care of ourselves, for a while. As we look in the mirror, we ask ourselves, how did this happen? The truth is we already know the answer. We didn't pack on that extra 20 pounds because we sat down one day and gorged on 100 pounds of ice cream along with 30 pounds of potato chips. It all started a long time ago, and it was just one little slip at a time. Habits, habits, habits, each one seemingly pretty harmless, but put them all together and here we are. Instant gratification, eating 1,000 calories for every 700 calories worth of physical exertion. Eating the quick out-of-the bag or box meal instead of the healthier meal prepared at home. But way worse than what we've done to ourselves is what we are doing or have already done to our children. There are very few if any of us that are not at least a little bit guilty of starting our kids down the same path that got us here. Some of us may think, 'well, I'm not in too bad of shape for a person my age,' and that may be fine for you. But given the choice for your children, wouldn't you want better than just "not too bad of shape?" We don't want to look at our teenage child and see an obese or pudgy or even the slightly out of shape kid, knowing that he or she could look much better and certainly be much healthier with a little exercise and healthier eating habits. And we don't want to look and see our child in their 20s, 30s, or 40s with a beer belly, with damaged skin due to sun tanning beds, facial scars due to acne problems from eating junk food, or just plain out of shape simply from laziness, when we know that we could have done better. You see, most of what we do to our body to make it less than it could have been was done a little at a time, starting with little bad habits that grew into a lifetime of bad habits, and most of where that child went wrong started with us.

So we screwed up. There's not a one of us who did it all right. Not every example we set for our kids growing up was the best. It would be easy to pass it off by saying, "We did the best we knew how," which in some cases may be the truth. Unfortunately, that won't make us feel any better as we see our kids repeating our mistakes. Fortunately, it isn't a done deal. We can still do better. The kids can witness their parents in their 60s living a more balanced and healthy lifestyle, putting an end to some of those bad habits and adopting better choices. It's not too late.

If we smoked or ate poorly and were overweight and unhealthy earlier in life and have since turned over a new leaf and have taken on more responsibility for our health and lifestyle, let's share it with our children and allow them to learn from our hard learned lessons. If we overspent and ran up a lot of debt to a point where we're now forced to pay for yesterday's mistakes, let the children know just how difficult it is to dig out of a hole in hope that they won't simply watch and follow our poor examples, but learn from us. Though we may be embarrassed by our actions, let them know how hard it is, let them know the mistakes you made and the consequences that ultimately followed.

Sometimes they can learn the lessons of a skinned knee simply by watching someone else suffer the pain of it. If you're ashamed of your stupid actions, admit to them and let them see the pain. Make your hard-learned lesson multiply. If you had to learn a lesson the hard way, why keep it to yourself? Save your children the time and grief by sharing the truth with them.

DON'T FEED THE SQUIRRELS

CHASING THE RABBIT

I'd love to give credit but I can't remember who wrote or where I read the story about the guy who went to visit his aunt. It went something like this: The guy goes to visit his aunt and the aunt has this dog lying in the corner of the kitchen, a greyhound dog, barely opening an eye to even acknowledge his presence. Some time passes and the aunt leaves to go to the market and get some things. The man starts talking to the dog, and to his amazement, the dog raises his eyelids and starts to talk back. After the usual introductions and some small talk the man learns that the dog came to live with his aunt after being retired at a young age from dog racing. The man asks him, "What, did you get too old to race and that's why you were retired?" The dog says "No, I actually had a lot of good years left in me." So the man asks, "Were you losing races and all washed up or what?" The dog says, "No, I was winning every race and making my owners a fortune." "So why did they let you go, why did they put you out to pasture?" The dog says, "Oh, they didn't let me go, I quit." The man then asks, "Were they not treating you well, not paying you enough, why did you quit?" "Oh no," says the dog, "they treated me great, gave me anything I wanted, in fact I was the most talked about dog around." So the man, bewildered by this time, asks "Why on earth did you quit?" The dog says, **"One day I figured out that the rabbit wasn't real."**

Now though I can't remember the book in which I read this story, and I'm not sure that it went exactly like this, out of an entire book in which I can't tell you the title, this little story stuck in my mind. This little piece of something much bigger hit home to me. Maybe any other time in my life, I'd have read on and never given this story a second thought, but at that exact time in my life, and possibly in no one else's life but my own, I could relate to that dog's story. So, to the unknown author of that story and as far as that goes to all authors out there: Isn't that what it's all about? If a reader can get just one thing out of your writing that will positively affect their lives, you've succeeded.

For most of my adult life I lived and breathed my business. Though I'd always tried to make it a habit to work hard and play hard and we always seemed to take a lot of short vacations and long weekends, I never seemed to be able to get my mind away from work. Being in the building business, we experienced many sharp ups and downs, and maybe it was due to continually experiencing those tough and then prosperous times that I seemed to always have business on my mind. Maybe it was living and breathing our business that allowed or caused us to continue to succeed while many, if not most of our competitors did not. It would seem that I could be floating down a river fishing or out on the golf course, having dinner with friends, always while driving, and from the time I fell asleep at night to the moment I awoke, business was on my mind. Was it the desire to succeed and win, or the fear of failing and losing? The one thing that seemed to never change from the days as a child picking bottles and earning pennies till the days when we were earning millions of dollars was that I was always thinking of and trying to make more money. Ironically, that really was never that important to me as much as it was a means of keeping score. Just like a runner may constantly strive to improve on his time, cutting just a few seconds off the mile or a golfer constantly trying to improve upon his game, keeping score and constant improvement seemed to be of utmost importance.

In my line of work, continuously building wealth was no different than the athlete maintaining and building muscle, always trying to be in better condition and more prepared to compete. In fact it was the wealth, savings, and strong financial condition that allowed us to not only survive but to thrive through the tough times when the financially weaker players were left unable to make it to the finish line.

People who have worked for a company for thirty years and brought home a paycheck every two weeks have never experienced the stress and worries of a self-employed business person. I'd spent most of my life with everything on the line, remembering many sleepless nights wondering how I got myself in the position I was in, how I was going to pay my suppliers and employees, and of course the banks. It seemed that about every time housing sales were booming and everything was looking very rosy, the market would crash, and there we were again, except each time the numbers were much larger and our worries much bigger. We had grown from building 10–15 homes a year to consistently building in the neighborhood of 250 per year. That equates to about a house a day for every working day of the year. We continued to do pretty close to the same number for quite some time, of course with a short downturn in 2008 to regroup, and in doing so for such a long time, there came to be several hundred people from employees to the supply chain and subcontractor base who depended on our continued business for their incomes. There had come to be many small businesses that had been built around our business and existed almost, if not entirely, due to our work.

In the years following the financial meltdown of 2007–2008, we seemed to have the market to ourselves, but I could see that it would soon come to an end and business would get more difficult, and with that, a lot riskier. We had been through the good times and then the bad several times throughout the years and we were coming out on top again, but things were about to change and I had to ask myself, 'do I really have it in me to go another round?'

My son would sit down across the desk from me almost daily and discuss different deals, real estate purchases, and the upside or downside. He would show me his analysis of a particular project, sometimes very detailed, including the projected costs in dollars as well as time and the known unknowns, and sometimes he simply scribbled on a legal tablet but in a form that he and I could understand; we were making multi-million dollar decisions sometimes on a daily basis based on scribbled figures on a single sheet of paper, yet we knew exactly what we needed to know to evaluate the upside versus the risk. Many times the deciding factor would come down to the expenditures in time more than dollars, mainly because our limitations were tied so closely to both. There was no bank financing available and frankly, by that time we were so disillusioned and lacking trust in the banks and the constraints that our government had placed on them, we were pretty much OK going it on our own. We had an enormous, but still limited amount of money to work with and we knew that we were even more limited on time, as this window of opportunities was soon to close. To plan for and properly provide for a pipeline of continued business for future years would have meant committing ourselves for at least another six years or more since land development is a very lengthy process and the dollars we would have to commit to that could put us right back where we had been so many times before, with sleepless nights and at-risk again.

One day, while sitting in my office, my son said to me, "Dad, what are you doing? You have more money than you can ever spend, and you really don't have a need to go out there and risk it. Besides, one day the government is just going to take most of it away from you anyway."

I was like the greyhound dog looking at that rabbit he'd been chasing all of his life. I remember telling my wife, Erin about my desire to shut down our business and just quit. She said, "Are you sure you want to do that?" And then immediately with a worried look and almost teary eyed she said, "What about all the people?" I said, "If not now, then when? Five years from now, ten years from now? It will always be tough, whether now or later." You see, for both Erin and I, the people part of the business had always been the absolute best part about being in business and at the same time, ironically the worst and most difficult thing. One thing that changed in recent years with our growth, as well as the overall change in the business, is that I was no longer as closely tied to a lot of the people in the field. There was a time that I could go out on any jobsite and talk to and know the names of every person on the site, from our own personnel to the delivery truck drivers, and most of the employees of all of our subcontractors. More recently most of our hiring was done by our project managers, so I could no longer be sure of the names of my own employees, and the hundreds of other people who were constructing our houses. For the most part, we didn't even speak the same language.

No, the fun was gone, and it seemed as though the reasons for chasing, living, breathing, and building the business, which I'm sure were once very legitimate and important, were now just much less so. Not wanting to waste another day, we set out a one-year plan to build out what we had and shut our business down. We gave everyone one year advance notice so they could make plans. We incentivized key personnel to stay to the end. We were taking a highly profitable, fine-tuned operation and just shutting it down, not selling it, not downsizing, just shutting down. People thought we were nuts.

My wife and I, being in our mid-fifties, could have another 30 active and productive years ahead of us, so what were we going to do? Well, those next chapters of our lives had yet to be written, but one thing was for sure, enough was enough and it was time to change it up. I once heard a saying, "**Retire when you have enough and have had enough.**" Well, we certainly had had enough. Besides, this was not retirement for us, since we still had other things going on that required a dozen or so employees, but we were able to put our main business to rest, and hopefully be able to get a little rest ourselves.

So, that's the story of how the rabbit stopped being real to me. I wonder how many others out there started out decades ago with all sorts of incentives and reasons for doing what they did on a daily basis, and today just keep going through the moves, week after week, year after year, literally spending their entire lives chasing things that are no longer of the same importance to them. My hat's off to anyone who from the start either stumbled into or had vision enough to start at an early age in an occupation or position that filled the purpose then and still does today.

Most people start out working at a job or an occupation to earn money because they need to provide for themselves and their family. But for many, I won't say lucky people, since for the most part, we make our own luck, many people through foresight and hard work have succeeded in providing for their young families and then at some point that job is done, the kids are grown and your reasons for getting up in the morning and going out into the world may have changed, but you still go through the same gate, follow that same routine, with little thought as to what else is out there with your name on it. The stay-at-home mom is an obvious example of when the children and the household were the rabbit, they were very real and worthwhile, but as the kids are off to school, and she now has free time or they are grown and move away, there can and most likely should be great change ahead. Too many people struggle with and never adjust and just seem to continue to try to keep things the same when circumstances are such that it is impossible to stay the same, the rabbit is no longer real.

It is very typical for a company to employ a sales representative that may be in his or her late 20s or 30s, since they seem to do very well in relating with the customer base, which in many cases are in the same age group. Years go by quickly and the sales rep finds himself in his late 40s or 50s, with his client base seemingly getting younger and younger to a point where he no longer can relate to his customers as he had in the past. Unfortunately, it does no good to keep beating a dead horse, and it may be time to move on. There are a lot of reasons why whatever you were doing, which made sense in the past, no longer does. Most people stay longer than they should, and most people don't see it coming or properly prepare. For anyone who depends on the strength of their body or their looks to earn a living, be aware that your best earning years may have already passed and you better start planning for yourself because no one else will.

Each one of us would do well to frequently evaluate how we spend our work time as well as our leisure time to see if they really bring us the same joy, or if they serve the same purpose that they once did. A wasted life is a terrible thing, and today is a huge part of that life as well as tomorrow and the next day. **In these days of "green living," people are keenly aware of reducing waste when it comes to a drop of water, a piece of newspaper, or a plastic bottle, but then they'll waste the most valuable resource available to them: a life. And life is something that we won't get a chance to recycle and use twice.**

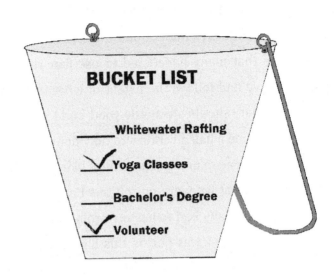

NUMBER EIGHT, THE ULTIMATE SIN

Those raised as Christians learn early about the Seven Deadly Sins. Even at the same time as parents are preaching to their children, most are also laying down the rules of the household, one of them being, "**Do as I say, not as I do.**" The Catholic Church has broken down the sins into Venial Sins, those that people can be forgiven for and live to see another day, and Mortal Sins, those that may condemn a person to "eternal damnation." I'm not sure if I could give a definition of eternal damnation, nor am I qualified or versed enough in any religion to speak intelligently enough to delve too deeply into this area. For me personally, as well as most of the people I know, well, we are what we were told we are. I just always thought I was a Christian, even though I never regularly attended any church for any period of time. As a child, all I knew of Jews or Judaism is that the Nazis killed a lot of them for no reason. Growing up in a rural area, I don't think I ever ran across a Muslim or Buddhist person, so you might say that my religious teachings or options were pretty limited. Even though I heard but never understood the term, "The fear of God," and it seemed to me that many have tried to use fear through religion to get people to believe and follow, the extent of what I took out of my limited teachings was that I should always do good, and I should never do bad.

It's taken me a half a century to fully define what that means. It's a no-brainer for anyone to understand things like "thou shalt not kill," but to really figure out what we were put on this Earth for and act accordingly, well, I found that I really had to use my brain to get to the bottom of that. And fortunately, when I was put on this Earth, I was given one of those. We all know that there have been more wars fought and blood shed due to religious beliefs or differences in beliefs than for any other reason. People don't understand others so they fear them. Just one great freedom we enjoy in this wonderful country of ours is the freedom of religion. You don't have to believe in what I do, but the law says that you can't discriminate or persecute me because of my beliefs either.

All Biblical writings are left to be interpreted by man, so when it comes down to it, at the best, we have stories and lessons that have been handed down and handed down again, written and revised, so the best thing a person can do is to use their brain and think independently.

We could talk about the Deadly Sins until we're blue in the face, but I've figured out on my own, simply using my brain, what I consider to be the absolute biggest sin of them all. It is said that all humans are sinners and I believe that to be true.

The biggest sin that man can commit is to waste a life. I'm not talking about taking of a life; I'm talking about not fully making the most of the one thing given to each of us and only us, our life. We were given this amazing human body complete with a brain, feelings, and a conscience. Regardless of a person's beliefs, what or how they envision their god or gods, and whether they regularly worship or not, I can't imagine anyone on this Earth believing that all this just appeared on its own. Beyond that, it is only from books that people extract or are taught whether we're constantly being watched over, or what will happen to us when our life on this Earth ends. One thing we can all agree on is that we were each given one life, at least that we know of. From the time we're born, everything we do will affect the length, and more importantly quality of our one life. There are those who will say that the best way to maximize the life you have is to spend it worshiping and spreading the word of God, and others who would say to dedicate every moment to helping others. There are those who feel guilt if they possess too much while others may be going without. My thoughts are that a person is best to do what pleases them most. In fact, in many cases, the person who seems the most giving, who always seeming to sacrifice for others, is in reality doing so for him or herself because giving brings them joy.

Many times a school paper is judged on several factors, with a different emphasis or percentage put on different aspects: 10% for structure, 20% for grammar, 5% for penmanship, etc. What if there really is to be a judgment day at the end of each of our lives, and the period that we spent on Earth is to be judged with the largest emphasis on how well we utilized the sacred thing we were given, our life? Then, go a little farther, and what if we're judged on a curve, comparing us with all the other human beings' performances, maybe even past and present? You must admit that this makes as much sense as any other means of judgment yet to be explained or fully understood. Though people have been taught and expected to believe that "faith" and "belief" are the most important part of life, using the human brain given to us, one could question if more may be expected of us, something that may have been lost through interpretation or even omission. Why would we be judged or graded on a curve? Well, it seems impossible that anyone would get 100%. In fact, when you really think about it, the top scores may come in closer to 20 or 30% because I can't believe there is a human being out there that hasn't wasted some valuable time, and greatly underperformed in some or many areas of their life as compared to their full human capabilities.

There's a country song by George Strait that goes, "I'm not here for a long time, I'm here for a good time." We've all seen people who seem to have it all, do it all, or know it all. We've also seen people who seem to just exist. There can be a person sitting on their couch at 90-years-old that hasn't lived as much life as the 25-year-old. Living life to its fullest for one person may be completely different and of no interest to another. One person's idea of an absolute and full life may entail learning and soaking in as much knowledge about any one thing or about everything, while the next person's goal is to see the most places, experience the most things, etc. Right or wrong, at the end of it all, whether there turns out to be a judgment at the end or not, I'd like to think I could at least look back at the end and have as few regrets as possible. Some people fear death so much that they are afraid to really live.

If you've ever worked or worked out really hard until you're hot, sweaty, and nearly exhausted, or just crashed down at the end of a totally exhilarating day or activity, you probably can remember the good feeling you felt at the end. I'm thinking of a sunny day, about 5:00 in the afternoon, staggering up the bank of an Idaho river and plopping my aching body down on the river rocks, looking up at the sun thinking, '**how can I feel so good when I hurt so bad?**' I'd just spent the entire day kayaking with my son and a good buddy down rapids that were so far beyond the capabilities of the three of us that I was just happy and amazed that we had survived. I heard my buddy say as he crawled from his boat, "I don't ever want to do that again," as my son, who was then in his mid-twenties said, "That was the most fun I've ever had." I ached from the top of my head to the tip of literally every toe, couldn't move my left arm, as it had cramped up earlier to a point where I was left to navigate the last few bends in the river one handed, yet as I lay there on that rocky riverbank, I was smiling and just couldn't stop laughing.

Now, what if after about 70, 80, or 90 years or however many years we survive, we could lay back and enjoy that same feeling and say, "That was the most fun I've ever had," and "I don't ever want to do that again?" I'm talking about looking back on an entire life as if it were that day in awe and in disbelief, smiling with every ache, laughing with every memory of the pleasures and the fears, the successes and the failures.

Obviously every day of a person's life can't be life threatening and body pounding, and sometimes the absolute best way to spend the day is simply a down day, a day of rest and recuperation, maybe with a good book, or staring out at the scenery, otherwise it undoubtedly would be a much shorter life as we probably wouldn't continue to tempt fate indefinitely. Sometimes, the best day is a good hard day at work, or maybe a day when everything went wrong and you are hugely disappointed but with it came a good lesson.

If "greed" is one of the big sins, is it wrong for a person to want to live forever, just to want more and more? Shouldn't we each be happy and thankful for however long we get, and with that in mind want to make the very most out of however long that turns out to be? When people talk about how they want to live to be 90 or 100, I have to quietly think to myself how lucky I am and how I think I may have already lived a pretty full life, and that every day from here on out is a bonus. That's why I hope at the end that we get judged or graded on a curve, because I watch people and I think that most people are not scoring very well right now.

So as I'm sitting here writing, reflecting on my life of 56 years, with the thought that the biggest sin a person can commit is to waste a life, like everything else I seem to do, I reach for the calculator: 20,454 days, that's how many are in 56 years, including leap years. But, even if I subtract the first sixteen years, for which I shouldn't be accountable since I was just a kid, that leaves over 18,000 days. Now, assuming that a human body and mind require about 8 hours of rest or sleep each day, I come up with approximately 208,000 hours that I was responsible for, and hopefully didn't waste. So, let's see, that day on the river was about 8 hours on the water, but you know, I spent the time that morning as well as the rest of the afternoon and well into the evening with good friends and family, so I'm going to count all of the hours that day, the entire day as "not wasted." Just like most good things, you had to be there, so that day on the river was part of a seven-day float trip, every one of them well spent, but it took a day each way driving to get there as well as getting home, not so fun. Travel days, I don't care where you're going, are never much fun. What they are is productive, after all, you could never have accomplished the great day without the effort put forth to get there. This is no different than the commute back and forth to work, so I've got to think that the time spent in the quest of any worthwhile action is certainly not wasted.

I'm in no way suggesting that a person's life was not fully utilized or any of it wasted simply because they didn't spend every minute having fun and enjoying life. No, quite the opposite. Most anything in life needs to be earned. Typically a person spends their early years learning and being educated, the next period of their lives working to support their life, raising and supporting a family, and contributing to society. Then, the later years are expected to be the years where we no longer have to work so much, and hopefully live off the nuts we put away. All along the way, however, we have all of those hours in each of those days, seven days a week. I can't help thinking that the absolute best way to have spent each and every one of them is a balance: a balance of learning and improving, working and earning, and celebrating and having fun. We've all heard the saying "All work and no play makes Jack a dull boy." And it works both ways, a person who does nothing but play, whether it be in their childhood or adult years, will find themselves passed up and empty-handed, wondering why others are enjoying a fuller life later on.

Go back in time and envision the way people used to live. Most had to work a lot harder and certainly a lot longer hours simply to survive. There was a time when a person would have to go out into the forest, then chop and carry wood if they were to heat their home or cook their food. The food, it wasn't just there, they had to grow it or kill it. They had to pack their water, can and preserve their winter's provisions, milk the cow, and butcher the chickens. They would spend the entire year preparing for the winter just to survive the season, and then it started all over again. In many parts of the world, this is still the way they live. Today, at least in this great country, we typically have someone who does each of these things for us, providing us with electricity and gas, food and shelter, and for some, everything right down to the cleaning of the house or the mowing of the lawn is done for them. In order to make this happen, at least the way it's supposed to work, is that each one of us has our part in the system. I might have been the guy that constructs the housing, while there is another guy who never has to worry about that since he works on cars and he takes care of my car and the car that belongs to the guy that works for the electric company. The farmer who provides the produce to the supermarket lives in a house and drives a car that he didn't build and that he doesn't have to repair. This is the way it has worked for thousands of years. In this country, from the Native Americans who were here before any of us, to the early settlers, the workload has been shared, with someone out hunting the game while another was back at the village tanning the hide and preparing the meal. Over time people would figure out that, if the blacksmith in town was better and faster at shoeing the horse, then a person could trade their service, whatever they had to offer, for his services. People would congregate on Sunday after church and share food and drink, dance and play music, but the rest of the week it was early to bed, early to rise, and everyone worked, everyone did their part.

Today in this country we have a very small minority of the people doing the chores, and the rest enjoying the fruits of others' labor. And we're not just talking about just getting by. Half the nation's people don't work at all, a large segment of the rest take much more than they contribute, but the expected minimum lifestyle is the same. How do you suppose that would have worked in a Native American tribe or out on the prairie in the frontier days? I'm thinking there would have been a lot of people dying from starvation and frostbite.

Still, today there are plenty of places in the world where a person needs to spend the bulk of, if not the entire day working simply to ensure their survival, leaving very little time for fun, playing, or entertainment. So come judgment day, I don't think a person's life is to be measured by how much fun they had, how much good they did, or how much they worked, but rather, if they maximized their limited time on this Earth to the best of their ability.

One common factor in nearly all religious teachings is the ability to be forgiven, repentance, and that short of the big sins, we can come to our senses, realize the error of our ways and try to make amends and still find our way through the pearly gates. That would explain why so many people find religion late in their lives. So, for any of us who believe that the wasting of a life or the failure to maximize that life is the ultimate sin, and reflecting back we can see at least some times when we didn't fully utilize the gift we were given, there is still hope. Do we have to go in the box and confess to the priest, "Father, I have sinned," kneel privately and pray, promising to do better, or can we use the brain given us and spend every day, today, tomorrow and the rest of them in such a way that the amazing human form was meant for? After all, aren't we all capable of so much more than we've been doing?

I drive four different types of vehicles built by four different manufacturers. Each vehicle has a different navigation system, and each is loaded with the latest technical advances that the manufacturers feel consumers want. These vehicles are capable of so much, where I have a tough time operating them beyond just the basics. There are buttons and features that I've never used, and frankly, am afraid to touch. I can look around the perimeter of my computer screen on my desk after working on it day after day and not understand 90% of the features and capabilities available to me. Anything from a phone to a toaster, the salesman will tell me, "You can do this and you can do that," and I'm thinking, 'Well, maybe you can do that but I can't do that.' The point is that every day we go through our routines, using just a fraction of and experiencing a fraction of the things available to us today. Many, if not most of these things are not necessarily readily available to people in other parts of the world, or are they? The reality is that just about anything and everything is available to us and most people on this Earth, though they may never even be or become aware of it. People simply sit around and complain while others go out and seek things out. **A good example is that the came-to-America Americans go to great efforts to see, learn of, and enjoy the life they're living in this country, while a large percentage of the born-American Americans are missing out while it's all here, right under their noses.** Now that's a sin.

THE OTHER SEVEN AND THE ANTICHRIST

The Bible speaks of an Antichrist without giving us much of a description, leaving us to be aware and keep our eyes open. Though these are not beliefs that I share, in recent years the most common names that have come up are George W. Bush, Barack Obama, and yet in past years I can remember some people claiming that Bill Gates must be the dreaded Antichrist. There were people who despised Mr. Gates simply for what he had. People just couldn't understand how a man could have so much and not give it to others. Forget all the good the man did to promote the lifestyle and further the evolution of not only the American people but those of the entire world. Forget the millions of jobs that have been created, again across the world, due to the innovation and visions of the early founders of Microsoft. The lazy and ignorant people who were putting him down were just like the Barack Obamas of today, "it's not fair," "equality," "equal pay," "have and have not's." Yes, there were many millionaires created in those early Microsoft years. You couldn't say Bill Gates was stingy or even greedy when he was creating jobs where people were highly compensated, many of whom have gone on to spread their wealth around in the form of charities and more job growth. People were not listening in those early years when Mr. Gates was saying, "Someday I'll give most if not all my money away." He didn't waiver, he stuck to his plan, and today he and his wife, Melinda, have not only pledged to give most, if not all of the fortune away, they have created The Gates Foundation. The Gates Foundation is the largest charitable organization in the history of the world. You see, Bill realized that he could give a dollar away to a person who is sitting on his couch complaining, and come tomorrow no one would be better off, or he could use his unique abilities to build that dollar into a thousand dollars and then into a million dollars and then he could really make a difference, and what a difference they are making! And could he or would he have done or been able to do what they are doing today without his wife Melinda? Who knows, but together they have and are continuing to create an institution that is investing billions of dollars to do everything from eradicating diseases to providing food and water to children in nations where people really don't have the ability or opportunities to help themselves. But still to this day, the Gates don't seem to be too interested in giving handouts to the people in our nation who have become conditioned to getting free stuff. No, they are concentrating where they believe they can truly make the most difference. In fact, these people have been doing such good and in doing so, set such an example for so many other wealthy people in this nation as well as other nations in the world that many others are pledging their fortunes in similar directions and even joining in and donating to the Gates Foundation. Hmmm, Bill

Gates has certainly raised the curve, don't you think? I don't know about the rest of you, but I like a good challenge.

The Seven Deadly Sins

Wrath: Intense anger; rage; fury

Greed: Excessive desire, especially for wealth, avarice

Sloth: Laziness; idleness

Pride: An unduly high opinion of oneself; haughtiness; arrogance

Lust: Bodily appetite; especially, excessive sexual desire; overwhelming desire; to feel an intense desire

Envy: Disconnect and ill will about another's advantages or possessions; desire for something that another has.

Gluttony: The habit or act of eating too much

Though biblical references leave plenty to be interpreted, we're usually left to view things through Webster's definition. So, I brought up people's thoughts towards people like George W. Bush. I think we have to give the man a break. George W. may have found The Lord and became a born-again Christian conveniently at a time that coincided with his entry into the political arena, much like the majority of other politicians, after all, all they have to do is read the polls to see what gets votes. And as far as his great leadership abilities and accomplishments, he ranks right up there with Jimmy Carter as being one of the worst presidents in at least the recent history of this country. Putting aside our deepening involvement in the Middle East, especially Iraq, under his direction, which I just don't understand, like Jimmy Carter, I think he really was and is a good man and truly did have the good of the American people in mind with every action. Running the country is surprisingly similar to running a large company, as the team you build and people who you surround yourself with will undoubtedly be the difference between long-term success and failure. It's too bad George W. was not strong enough to have chosen better than the likes of people like Dick Cheney and Donald Rumsfeld, and maybe, just maybe we would have avoided much of the bloodshed and military waste that was set in motion under his command. Aside from that, and of course his utter inability to speak and come across as the intelligent man I'm sure he is, at least, morally he set a decent example for the people of this country. He encouraged hard work and job growth. Unlike a large percentage of other politicians both past and present, you never read about any sex scandals or "Monica Lewinski" soiling his reputation. From Bill Clinton's Monica Lewinski among many others, Senator John Edwards, to Representative Anthony Weiner, and even the much admired President John F. Kennedy, and as far as we can go back in history, it seems as though the very people who are in positions to lead and set examples behave like most parents, "Do as I say, not as I do." You might say that many of these high ranking individuals are promoting bad behavior, telling people to throw caution to the wind, and don't even think about consequences; so much for avoiding that deadly sin of lust.

Lust: President Obama has done just about everything within his power to promote every deadly sin except for this one. Maybe that's simply because he is just so much in love with himself. Most in the know would say he is without a doubt the narcissist of all narcissists. That, coupled with the fact that he spends most of his time in front of the camera, maybe he just hasn't had the time to get himself in that kind of trouble, yet.

Envy and Greed: We are living in a time when we have more people in this nation contributing less and receiving more. Our leader has managed to rile up the masses and get so many concentrated not on what they have and should be thankful for, but on what their neighbors have and thinking, "Why not me?" People are, at the very least, naïve and gullible to continue following this guy. How can you follow a guy who only preaches the negative, reminding people of what they don't have, what they're not getting, instead of setting an example and steering the great people of this nation toward all the possibilities available to them through hard work. This president has single-handedly led millions of people down a nasty path, a sinful path.

Pride: His constant displays of arrogance are broadcast daily across the nation for all to see and emulate. His face is either in the camera or on our screen more than any past leader, telling lies and promises of working across the aisle and uniting others as he at the same time proceeds to tout the "power of the pen," basically alienating even his own party members.

Wrath: Obama has separated our nation in a few short years, reversing a momentum of unification that has progressed for over 200 years to a point where a large portion of the population are now angered and enraged, not that different than what we see in countries like Iraq, Afghanistan, Egypt and other places lacking any sort of unified leadership.

Sloth and Gluttony: This president, with complete disregard for the good of our nation and out to promote his own personal agenda, has done everything within his power to reverse what once made this country great, the ideas and incentives to work hard, contribute, become self-reliant and productive. He has nearly ruined this nation as well as its reputation, leaving us to deal with half the population being lazy, inactive, idle takers, happy to wait at the feeding trough expecting the few to feed the many.

IF IT MOOS LIKE A COW

Everybody knows where milk comes from, but few have ever thought about how it gets extracted from the cow, and even fewer realize that they themselves are being milked every day of their lives. The majority of the people in this nation are living the life of a cow.

Growing up in a rural area, our family raised chickens for eggs and meat, and had a few cows for beef but never had any milk cows. Dad would, however, buy an occasional milk cow from the neighboring dairy farmers or at the stock auction to send to the butcher to be ground into hamburger. Thankfully we never had milk cows, as that was a tough life for a kid growing up on a dairy farm. There were several dairy farms around our place, and though I worked for those farmers, mending and building fences as well as bringing in hay and cleaning barns, I never had anything to do with the milking of the cows. Back then a farmer could earn a decent living with about 100 cows, which for most family-run operations is about all they could handle. Like most farming operations, dairy farming requires long hours and a lot of hard and dirty work. Generally milk cows get milked twice a day and it's extremely important to have a very consistent schedule so as to get the most production. Typically the cows would get milked every 12 hours, so that meant somewhere around 5:00 a.m., and then again 5:00 p.m. Then, twice daily in the hours following the milking, a tanker truck would show up and take delivery of the milk just to return about 12 hours later in order to provide fresh milk to the markets. This happened 7 days a week. The cows never took a holiday. No, they gave milk in the morning and then again in the evening, every day, including Christmas and Thanksgiving Day. And as you might expect, as they gave milk twice each day, they were fed not three times a day but twice a day.

Whether it was 50 years ago when I was witnessing the cows heading for the barn and milking parlor, or today, I would guess that if I were to go to any dairy farm around 15 minutes before milking time, I would see a single file line of cows, one following another, usually with the same lead cow in front, filing into the barn until the last enters. They do this voluntarily, without being asked or forced. They then proceed to put their head through a vertical metal bracket called a stanchion that clamps around their neck to restrain them, at which time they know they'll be fed, all the time while someone from behind will be fondling their private parts and hooking up a sucking machine that will extract every drop of milk. Once the "Feeders" have gotten what they want from the cows, they'll unlock the neck restraints and one-by-one in single file, the herd will return to the field, just to return 12 hours later to be restrained, fed, and milked again, and they do this because that's what they've always done. And if one day a particular cow starts putting out less of a yield than a new cow may be able to do, then the old cow is sent to the meat market and made into hamburger.

Every animal, from a dog to a hamster, can be trained to do tasks by getting it so used to receiving a treat or something it desires until it becomes automatic, and the animal performs the task without thought.

During those same youthful years many of us kids would attend "Children's Meeting" every Friday night. An old bus would pull up and take us to a little church building where we would learn about the Bible and sing songs. At the end we each got a candy bar, rode the bus home, and come next Friday, you could bet we'd be there ready and waiting, I suppose because that's what we always did. The funny thing is that the people putting on these meetings and spreading the word of God were the same farmers who had their way with the cows. They learned that if they fed the cows, getting them conditioned and dependent on those feedings, they would come along willingly and one would follow the other. So, if hay and grain would work with the cows, it made sense that chocolate bars would work with children, and it did. Thankfully these were good people with good intentions, and all they really wanted to accomplish was to get us hooked on the religion they wanted us to learn. Over the years we have learned of countless religious cults that, for little more than a candy bar have been able to lead large groups of people into doing things from suicide to all sorts of evil deeds. Even though I got out, I often wonder if there may be still some followers that are eating the candy.

Those meetings were actually good for me, as I learned a lot, and as far as the cows go, well I think it probably works out OK for them since you know, there are really no other opportunities out there for a milk cow, and besides, that's all they have ever known along with their parents and their parents.

In the case of the cows, the "Feeder" is the farmer, and in the case of the kids and the candy bars, the "Feeder' was the preacher, one and the same, but throughout our society we have the "Feeders" and the followers. The "Feeder" maybe the government, and in many cases things have evolved to a point where the "Feeder" is much bigger than the government, it is "the system." Just like the farmer has learned that he just has to get that first cow to head to the barn and the rest will follow, our government knows that all you have to do is set a system where people are fed, and like a dog rolling over, people will do as expected.

It's no accident that our great nation has become a gluttonous nation of consumers, a consumer society with the majority of our economy reliant on consumer spending. The sad thing is that a lot of people reading this may not even realize that this is not a good thing. Our nation not only survived but prospered for 200 years with a capitalistic system serving it just fine. People worked, bought, and traded services and products, prices of goods and services found their proper place on their own and people were rewarded for hard work and ingenuity. Just like the cows, people did as they had always done, as their parents and their parents had done. Even our government in past years did as they were supposed to, they stayed in line just like the cows, performing their expected functions, assessing taxes, paying their bills and returning to the barn just like the cows.

What do you suppose would happen if one day the cows made their way into the barn, stuck their heads into the stanchions, and there was no feed, no hay, and no grain? There has always been feed there for them, and frankly I doubt the cows have ever considered that it wouldn't be there. I'm thinking it would take about 12 hours for there to be milk shortages, that's a no-brainer, but what would happen to the cows? What would they do? They have spent their entire lives getting fed, getting milked, returning to the field to graze on grass just to return and do it all over again. This is all they have ever known. This is what they were taught by the elder cows and on and on.

We've got an entire nation of people who have never wondered or worried about what would happen to them or their family members when they stick their head in the stanchion and there is no feed.

DON'T FEED THE SQUIRRELS

BANKING DAY – IT'S THE SMALL THINGS

I'd love to give somebody a pat on the back but I don't know who was responsible. Maybe it was the superintendent of the school district, maybe the members of the local PTA, but I've got a hunch it was the greedy bankers. I say that jokingly, because what we think of as the greedy bankers today are not the same as the local bankers back then. Back then, the guy sitting behind the desk at the corner bank got to know people, their families, and he really was there for the community. If he was giving a loan, he was looking across the desk at the person he would expect to repay that loan. And that loan was probably made up of funds collectively assembled by the same community. It was an accumulation of small deposits, many times $10 or $20 at a time. In fact, when I was in elementary school back in the 1960s, once a month my teacher would remind the class that "Tomorrow is banking day." The next day we would show up with our nickels, dimes, and sometimes quarters, and we would get a brown envelope with our name and account number on it. We would put whatever change we had saved up over the month in that envelope. We then had a deposit book with a ledger to record our savings deposits.

For some reason, I would look forward to banking day. As small as it was, it gave me such a great feeling when I would look at that savings book and see that I was getting ahead. Each month I would deposit just some of my change, and watch that number grow. Then I would get a statement that would show not only the deposits I had made but miraculously the balance had increased even more. The bank was paying me interest on the money stored there. Little did I know at the time, that my money really wasn't actually being stored in the vault at that corner bank but was probably being loaned out to some guy sitting across the desk from Mr. Banker. That interest being paid to me was like a pat on the back, a 'that-a-boy.' Watching that savings balance grow, whether it be a dollar or cents at a time, gave me a great feeling of accomplishment, which unknown to me at the time was not only a feeling, but a habit, and a lesson I would experience, repeat, and build on throughout my life. That feeling of getting ahead as opposed to falling behind was no different than today if I get on the bathroom scale and see that I've lost two or three pounds. I may certainly have yet to reach the weight I'd hoped for or intended to be at by this time, but boy it feels good to be going in the right direction. Each day, I'd been conscious of everything I put into my mouth, as well as the little extra effort put forth to get that additional exercise. It would have been so easy to get that burger and fries at the drive through, rather than taking a few minutes and preparing the salad and fruit. I could have easily sat on the couch and watched that hour-long reality show instead of going for a walk with my wife. No, I've done that, I've experienced the feeling of looking at the scale that went the other way. It's not good. It seems like such an uphill battle, especially when I think, 'what the heck am I doing?' Each one of us experiences these feelings, both good and bad, getting ahead and falling behind, almost every day, but do we learn?

I could have bought candy. Living in a rural area, our closest store was a couple of miles away and was a little corner country store with an owner operator. The store's owner was named Dell, so it was Dell's Store. Dell was always there. Back then we could buy penny candy. It was penny candy because it cost a penny. Bottled pop or beer came in returnable bottles, so when someone bought a bottle of Coke or Olympia beer, they would pay a cent or two additional for the deposit. When they returned to the store for the next purchase they could return the empties for credit or cash. Well, fortunately for us kids, not everyone valued those pennies like we did. People would roll down the window of their car or truck and toss them in the ditch. I rode my bicycle with a burlap sack for miles, scouring the ditches, picking up the empty bottles and bringing them to Dell at Dell's Store to exchange for cash, usually cents, not dollars. Some beer bottles were worth one cent, some pop bottles three cents, and once in a great while, the big find, a big pop bottle, worth a nickel. Sometimes I would venture out for a long day and travel to Len's Market, which was many more miles from home. That opened up all new territory for my bottle picking. Len's Market was owned and operated by Len. Len, just like Dell, didn't shutter or grumble when he saw me peddling up with the bag of dirty bottles, but instead counted them out with me, inspected them to ensure they weren't cracked or chipped, and we did our business. He always knew that after he handled all of the dirty bottles and paid me off, maybe a buck or so on a good day that I'd be buying not only some penny candy, but maybe a pack of bb's, or maybe even a bottle of pop. You could bet that was one bottle that wouldn't end up in the ditch. If I made a buck, I would spend part of it but rarely all of it, after all, it would soon be banking day. I might have been 10 or 11 years old, and when I got home for dinner that night, Mom or Dad never asked where I'd been all day. I guess they just figured it was like any other work day. Not to say that it was all work and no play. Between me, my brothers and sister, we had ample time to play as well as get into plenty of trouble. But especially in the summer months, there was no hanging around the house complaining that there was "nothing to do," or "I'm bored." We were gone from morning till evening, working or playing.

If it wasn't bottle hunting, it was peeling Cascara, trapping Muskrats for the pelts, bucking hay bales, or picking and selling berries. Cascara bark from the Cascara tree is used to make laxatives. So we would go for miles out in the woods climbing and peeling the bark off of these trees. We would take it home, lay it out to dry for weeks until it cracked and was ready to take to the feed store and sell. Who owned the trees whose property they were on, we didn't really know. Was it stealing? Probably, but we never really thought about it that way. Each one of us in my family found our way to earn a living as kids. I say 'a living,' since Mom and Dad were sure not going to be giving us any handouts. As a family, we all participated in raising a garden and animals for food, eggs, and meat, so we always ate well, but beyond that, we were expected to figure it out, as we did.

I always wondered why the bottles were there in the ditch. Not so much why someone would toss something with such value, but why someone hadn't already beaten me to it. Why hadn't one of the other neighbor kids been there and nabbed those bottles and gotten to that penny candy before me? Or why was the bark still on that tree when we got there to peel it? Could it have been that the other kids, even back then, were receiving handouts? Were they getting those extras like candy and bb's without having to figure out how to earn them? Most of them would also participate in banking day, sliding a couple quarters in their own envelopes. Were they being given those quarters?

Were the other parents so rich that they could just give their kids stuff for free? Well, as it turns out, not unlike our government handouts today, many of these other parents were providing these handouts by running their own deficits. You see, even back then, Dell and Len were running tabs for the people in the community. The neighbors would buy things throughout the month and tell Dell, "Put it on my tab." Dell had a little notebook with a running tab, and each month when people got their paychecks they would come in and pay for the stuff they had long since consumed, and come the day after payday, as you would expect, broke again, they would start the tab running. Dell was a fair guy but he was a businessman, so as you would expect, running a little country store, his prices were just a little higher than those at the grocery store in town. Mom and Dad got to know Dell very well over the years but their purchases from his store were pretty much limited to convenience, when they had forgotten something or a quick bottle of pop. Their grocery shopping was done at the B & M Grocery store in town. Others who were running a tab were buying a much larger percentage of their groceries where they could get credit, and as a result were paying more and getting less. Furthermore, they could never buy and own their food. They were always eating food that wasn't paid for. What's worse is that it seemed as though since they were just putting it on the tab, and they weren't actually peeling off the hard earned dollar, they tended to buy some things that we never saw in our house. But did we go without? No, once in a while, Dad would come home with a tub of ice cream. When I say tub, that's exactly what it seemed like, since it was 2-1/2 gallons, unlike the little half-gallon cartons the others purchased on credit at Dell's. Mom and Dad bought in bulk, and probably not the good stuff, but to us, boy it was good, and when we had a bowl of ice cream or ice milk, or whatever they could afford, we had a bowl, a big bowl. What I didn't know at the time is that it was paid for and Mom and Dad must have had that same great feeling of 'getting ahead' as I got when putting those coins in the banking envelope. When they had the freezer filled for the winter with meat and vegetables, and canning jars were stocked full, they were smiling. And looking back, I am sure that Dad hadn't spent the last penny of his dollar on that ice cream, because they had their own "brown envelope" system going on.

Just like a child learning to walk or talk, having to think about each step or word, soon these actions become habit, and without thought, the child is free to think about the next thing, and so on, and so on. Walking soon becomes so easy that before you know it that child is running and smiling the whole time. Developing good habits at an early age, whether it is work or savings habits, soon take no thought or effort. A person never un-learns, because it's just so much easier to do the right thing than the alternative. One might think just the opposite, and think that it would be easier to go over to the other side and start buying things before you can pay for them or working less and expecting more. But those people haven't felt the feeling, the feeling and relief of getting and being ahead instead of behind. Those people may get tired of the way they're living their life and come January 1, set out with a slew of resolutions to get in shape, physically or financially, just to fall back into the same old bad habits by the middle of the month. These old habits have become ingrained, like tobacco or heroin, and most people will just continue to use.

Inevitably the child that earns his or her own quarters and learns to spend some and save some, will later be the one loaning dollars to the ones who received the easy unearned quarters. Of course, they're going to have to listen to people complaining about inequality and the disparity between the rich and the poor. I guarantee that if I had one lone competitor out there in the bottle picking ditches, he would end up being my competitor today as well.

I recently had a friend tell me how she explained to her children about spending before they could afford to. Her son didn't understand how if you borrowed more money you would have less money. She explained that you could buy a couch today on credit, or wait till tomorrow when you can afford it and you could buy a couch and a coffee table for the same amount, when you consider the interest cost for buying on credit.

DON'T FEED THE SQUIRRELS

MISSED IT BY THAT MUCH

You don't know how close you came. It's all over the media, it controls our politics and elections, and it has recently driven a huge wedge between Americans, creating class warfare. Not just income inequality, but wealth inequality. How can some have such great wealth, anything they desire, and seem to have life so easy when others don't? There's no secret and its way simpler than anyone would believe. Get your lazy eyes and ears away from the reality shows and other distractions, open your eyes and look around.

There is a book titled *The Tipping Point* written by Malcom Gladwell. Many times when I read a book that I really like or truly get a lot out of, I'll buy more. I've bought dozens of copies of this book and handed it out to people who I felt would understand and benefit. *The Tipping Point* is about what it sounds like. Almost anything in life can be or get too far one way or the other, many times somewhat unnoticed until it reaches a point of no return or unsustainability. Look at our recent history; let's say the last hundred years, and you'll see booms and busts, wartime and peace, extreme conservatism to hugely damaging liberalism. Throughout history, great civilizations have been built and toppled, rarely due to any single event but due to little things adding up to a point where it all implodes, at which time the circumstances will then go so far in the opposite direction until they again reach a tipping point where something has to change. And it does. And it's usually not a pretty site or happy period of time.

Many people could be living the life that exists only in their dreams right now, and it's much easier than they can believe. In some cases it may have required one simple change, one simple good habit as opposed to a bad habit. Sometimes maybe a combination of a few single simple actions, and voila, life is good.

You can smoke a single cigarette, tell a single lie, or sleep in and miss work one morning, have unprotected sex without getting pregnant or contracting a disease. You can cheat on a test instead of studying and really learning the subject or any other shortcut you can think of. Any one of these examples, as well as many others can be life altering the first time; however, chances are you'll get away with it once. It'll seem pretty harmless, but what about the second, third, and fourth time? It quickly becomes habit. However, saying no can also become habit, without effort.

Any one of a thousand seemingly little things you've done in your lifetime can be and most likely are the reason you aren't living the life you long for and probably will never enjoy.

What if, as a young person, you were told, "Show up early and stay late," and you put that into practice? You may today be lying on a beautiful

Caribbean beach watching your beautiful spouse and children playing in the water without a worry in the world.

What if as a young person you had listened and taken it seriously when you were told, "The people you surround yourself with will have a great effect on the life you live." Open your eyes and look around. What do these people have going for themselves?

What if you'd have had the confidence to never worry about having the nicest things, or keeping up with the Joneses?

No one likes to take responsibility, but almost without exception, where you are today is your own doing, the same goes for that one-percenter who is paying the way for others or the scratch golfer who seems to make it look easy. We love to hate others who are doing the things that we didn't take the effort to earn or learn.

DON'T FEED THE SQUIRRELS

DID YOU SERVE YOUR COUNTRY?

I was playing cribbage one evening with a good friend and, as usual, our conversation got into politics and world issues. I would say this particular friend is even more opinionated than me, and though we agree strongly on a few issues, we both tend to think the other is half crazy with our views towards almost everything else, so much so that our wives sometimes step in to say "OK, that's enough." We've learned to agree to disagree and respect the other's views. So, this particular night, in the heat of the discussion, he comes out and says, "Dave, have you ever served your country?" And then he asked again, this time with a little more force and much louder, "Have you ever served your country?" I knew exactly what he was asking, and I also knew that he knew the answer, at least for what he thought he was asking. He was fully aware that I had graduated high school shortly after the military draft and the Vietnam War had ended, and that I went right to work and never enlisted in any branch of military service.

I did not answer his question, as it would have surely been a long drawn out discussion and one that I was sure that we wouldn't agree on. You see, he served in Vietnam back when many didn't have a choice whether to "serve their country" or not. Uncle Sam was grabbing young people by the collar just out of high school and putting them through a quick basic training and sending them off to Hell. Though he didn't talk about it often, he had told me a few stories. Nearly forty-five years ago he spent nearly a year in a combat zone. Now, that alone sounds pretty scary to me, I mean even if a guy was a desk jockey or jeep mechanic, being over there at that time must have been very tense, and I'm sure they each counted the days until they were back home to hopefully resume, or in many cases, start a normal life. But my buddy wasn't some guy that had spent his time pushing papers. He was assigned to a Navy gunner boat that went up the rivers and canals, shooting and being shot at. He was dropped into a place where he didn't want to be, at a time in his life when he must have been dreaming of a thousand other things he'd rather be doing. This was at a time when most people back home were not in support of what we were doing over there. I say "we," as most of the American people were saying that, yet I'm sure for those over there trying to survive till morning ducked down in that gunner boat, I doubt it seemed like "we." They were there serving their country, like it or not. So, I was not about to disrespect him by saying, "Yes, Jim, I've served my country for the last 35 years."

No, I'll never receive healthcare, retirement, dependent or survivor benefits; I'll never get preference over any other individual when seeking a Federal job or get a government guaranteed zero-down home loan. If for some reason after decades of working hard I should find myself homeless and in need of help, I will be way down on the list, basically at the end of the line for any assistance in finding shelter.

In times of war, our armed services personnel, in combat or not, are working to protect our way of life back home. I'm sure they hope and expect that someone back home is keeping it going so there is something to return home to, something worth fighting or working for. We may get the political spin about "weapons of mass destruction," or see pictures of the mistreatment of people in other countries to try to justify our involvement overseas, but then we hear people saying, "It's all about oil." Whether it is about oil or any other asset that we are trying to protect in an effort to continue the life we enjoy here, let's hope that whatever the reason, it is worth fighting for.

This country above all countries in the world has become a nation of consumers, with much of our economy, and most of our jobs dependent upon people being able to go to work, get a paycheck, and then go out and spend it. In doing so, they create the need for another worker, whether it be in the retail sector, transportation and shipping, or any of the services from legal to financial. The American way of life depends on commerce, on transactions, on each person being able to sell their product or service to another, thereby enabling more people to do the same. That way of life every day, day in and day out, the only way of life that most Americans alive today have known, is what our soldiers are fighting for and what they expect to come home to.

None of us want to believe that a country would really be at war for oil but if indeed that is the case, then what about the captain of the oil tanker, or for that matter the guy that works at the refinery or the truck driver that transports the refined gasoline to the station where we just expect we can pull up and fill up? Are they serving their country? Aren't there thousands of different positions or job descriptions around the country that are critically important enough, positions that, if somebody didn't do them, our country would be in utter turmoil?

All we hear these days is "There are no jobs." Well, I'll say it again and I'll say it as many times as it takes, JOBS DON'T MAKE THEMSELVES! These days, so many don't seem to understand that jobs don't just appear. They are surely ignorant to the difficulty and risk that an employer endures just to add one more job. Now I'm not implying that every person needs to be the employer, or that any particular individual's job is less important than another's, but let's face it, jobs and the resulting paychecks, taxes paid and collected, and value added are the lifeblood of this great country. And it doesn't have to be the owner or founder of a company who is responsible for the job growth and building of a community. There are countless people in most organizations that are responsible for creating and re-creating jobs and on-going commerce. Without these people there would be many more unemployed, much less tax revenue, and no money or resources for the support of our government or armed services.

There are somewhere around 21 million veterans in this country, some who have made a career of military service and others who served active duty for 8 years, 4 years, and some as little as 90 days. There are presently over 1.3 million active military personnel as well as over 800,000 reservists. We have been programed to think that all of these people are heroes, and since the September 11th attacks, we've been conditioned to consider every police officer and firefighter as a hero. Now, that's just not right, in fact all that does is significantly lessen the value of the word "hero." No, just a fraction of those who put on a uniform and collect a paycheck are true heroes. I don't think we can really truly start honoring the heroic acts and the people who have performed them until we knock it off. There are just as many bad cops or firefighters as there are bad truckers or lawyers. There are probably just as many bad people who serve or have served in the military as those who work in the local county courthouse or at the corner grocery store. Aside from bad or good, the vast majority of people are decent; not bad, but not necessarily a hero either. And of course a person would not have had to pull off heroic deeds to have served their country. **Just as we should be selective in the use of the word hero, maybe we should put into perspective the use of the phrase "serving your country."**

I believe that I've served my country and I'm proud of my service. There are thousands like me, who never wore a uniform, but have served their country well. We are the entrepreneurs, the job creators, the ones responsible for millions of dollars in taxes being created for the federal, state, county, and city governments that keep this country going. My wife and I have paid tens of millions of dollars in personal income tax alone. Though we typically had around 50 direct employees, our companies were responsible for thousands of jobs in the trades, from the delivery of lumber to the gravel pit and trucking, along with the carpet manufacturer and mortgage banker. All along the way, every shovel or shovel full, every foot of electrical wire or gallon of paint was bought, delivered, taxes were assessed, and the process would start all over again. The materials required to build the thousands of houses that we constructed to house thousands of families, most of them working families, came from all across the country with American workers, creating, transporting and invoicing for each and every piece. But what about the independent trucker who may have hauled our drywall from Georgia to Washington? This guy may have risked everything to buy his truck, worked long hours for years to pay for it, all along the way paying taxes on the truck and taxes on the fuel, finally earning a buck, and then paying much of it out to the different branches of government. This guy fed and supported not only his family, but also the nearly 50% that didn't put the same effort forth that he did. He gave and didn't take. Did the trucker serve his country? I've got to say, if the country is better off for him being here and he has contributed more than he received, certainly he served his country.

In a few short years under Barack Obama, this country has gone backwards one hundred years, losing the progress and momentum made as far as equal rights and discrimination, the very issues he promised and that his supporters believed he would protect. In 1920, women were finally recognized as equal enough to enjoy the basic right of the vote. The 1960s brought great change through the Civil Rights movement, and more recently there have been great strides toward the improvement of Gay Rights. Up until just recently, we were finally reaching a point where the majority of people in this country were more accepting of others, and less prejudiced than at any time in history. Then, along came Barack Obama, preaching the differences in classes, the differences in races, and even the differences in occupations. And "preaching" is exactly what he has done and millions of people followed him and believed his lies, no different than if he was a cult leader leading them to drink the Kool-Aid. No person, at least in this country, in the entire history of this country, has done as much damage and set us back so far and so quickly in the long hard and bloody fights for equality. I would like to think that it is not due to some dastardly evil plan to end this nation, but rather simply his narcissistic, self-serving desire to promote himself. And what better or easier way than through the voters, the gullible voters, many of them ignorant, lazy, "what's in it for me" voters, or ill-read, follow-the-herd voters.

Across the country, I am seeing huge campaigns to end veterans' homelessness. President Obama wants to spend over 1.5 billion dollars (in borrowed money of course) in 2015 alone, that's four times the amount spent in 2009, of course also in a year of record Federal deficits, to end veteran homelessness, with a portion of that to go towards keeping thousands of veterans from losing their homes. Let me get this straight. The government puts the carrot out and gets these people into homes they can't afford with zero down VA loans, and then when they get in trouble, as is inevitable, he wants to bail them out, at the same time as identical "bad loans" are still being made to the next veteran. My problem is not the concept of helping anyone, veteran or not; it's that we're seeing the singling out of a specific group again, and in doing so discriminating and leaving others behind. Because members of this group once, possibly decades ago, wore a uniform, many for a short period, maybe from the ages of 18–22, and because it has become politically popular to use the word "Veteran" and the many associated photo opportunities, this group is being singled out and given immense preferential treatment as compared to other individuals in this country. I thought we fixed most of these things back in the days of Lynden Johnson. And let's face it, this is nothing but "spin" and it's not limited to Obama now, as most political figures have figured out what's popular and what gets headlines and votes.

What if we were told the government was planning on borrowing billions of dollars to provide housing for truck drivers, school teachers, or software engineers, and everyone else was to be ignored? Would it be any different or worse to say only female school teachers or only white male truckers received a certain benefit? Oh, and in order to get the free housing or numerous other services that no one else will get, that school teacher doesn't have to be a school teacher, they just have to show that they spent at least 90 days in the classroom sometime in their life, maybe decades ago. No, I don't suppose that would generate nearly as many votes, now would it?

I'm in no way suggesting that any particular group is more or less deserving, or that given the resources, we shouldn't do everything within our means to help, but in this country, more than any country in the entire world, we must treat people equal and not discriminate for or against any particular group, otherwise what have all the people fought and worked for in the past?

At the same time President Obama and the Democratic Party have started down the road of brainwashing the people with the fallacy of women being treated unfairly in the work place and being paid only 77% of what a man is paid, which again has little truth or basis. Again, we dealt with this, and we have laws in place. But he will accomplish three things: (1) He will split the nation even more as he has become so good at; (2) He will distract the unknowing voters from the real issues long enough to get through the next election cycle, giving him plenty of camera time; and (3) Lastly but possibly the underlying reason behind this campaign, he will repay millions of dollars in campaign contributions by giving the trial lawyers a heyday in messing up the laws already in place to deal with any discrimination like this. It's these types of assertions that are causing many Democratic political figures to try to separate themselves from the president. Next, will he be out in front of the camera proposing that we make it illegal to cause a black man to sit in the back of the bus or drink from a separate drinking fountain? We've dealt with all of these things and for decades now, the American people were finally getting along.

People need to stop following like sheep and start thinking for themselves. We need to get back to acknowledging all of the people who serve the country, from the farmer who helps feed the nation to the teachers who educate our children. But let's not leave out the neighborhood banker or insurance agent simply because it's not popular. Simply put, if a person has given more than they've been given, then they have been serving their country. Draw a line down the middle of a paper and list the contributors vs. the takers and you'll find that the contributor side is short. Operating a household, a company, or a nation is not sustainable this way and it will soon change. Our country has made past promises to veterans just to fall far short. There are thousands of veterans dying while waiting for promised treatment in overburdened VA hospitals, so instead of following through with old promises, they shift our focus over to something more politically popular: "Let's give them housing," (which of course, we can't pay for).

The entire nation has been promised that their social security dollars would be there when they need them and that they are being put away in some safe social security fund, just to find out that has been another lie and the only way the promised benefits will be able to be delivered is to go out and borrow those dollars also. The politicians continue to blow every dime, promise us what it takes to kick the can down the road, and as soon as a sane one stands up and says, "Hey, we can't keep giving all this free stuff," they're gone and their career is over. So how can you blame them for staying quiet?

Oh, and all those promised Federal pensions, and the FDIC insurance on your bank account? Well, don't count on those being there either.

THE FIRST STEP

"Hello, I'm an American." That's how it needs to start. No person who enjoys an occasional drink ever walks into an Alcoholics Anonymous meeting. No that only happens long after the habit has become a problem, and even then most likely not on their own accord. A person rarely seeks out change or help until it has nearly ruined their lives and many around them, many times, because they haven't even realized or admitted to themselves that it is or has been problematic. So, after years of slowly making poor decisions, wasting a good share of the best and most productive years of their lives, reluctantly, they seek out help, not because they want to, but generally because they have simply reached a point where the destructive behavior can no longer continue. We've all seen it in the movies, the guy finally enters and sits down at the AA meeting, usually in the back row, and listens, as one after another, people stand up, announcing their name and saying, "Hello, my name is XXX, and I'm an alcoholic." The new person in the room realizes that he is not alone. In fact, most of these people standing up and discussing all the awful things that they've done and the mistakes they've made could just as well be telling his story. It seems that the only noticeable difference in the lives of these poor pathetic people and his own are that they are doing something about it. So, when the new person finally gets the courage up to go in front of the rest of the group, the first statement is always, "Hello, my name is James Smith, and I'm an Alcoholic."

Regardless of the problem in this or any other person's life, it will rarely get better and most likely get worse unless they first admit to themselves and others that it is a problem, and secondly, that they want change. The person at that first meeting rarely goes in there saying to themselves "I never want to take another drink." No, they are more likely to want to return to the time when they could drink socially, have a good time with friends, and be that fun-loving guy he still envisions himself to be. The overeater wants and needs to get the habit under control but can't imagine having to go completely without enjoying food. The over spender may have seriously messed up his or her life along with their family's lives, and needs to adopt less destructive habits, but couldn't imagine going the rest of his or her life without making a purchase. I think we all know that once an alcoholic, always an alcoholic, which means that one may never be cured and one may never take another drink without falling right back into the same if not even worse conditions. The same goes for most drug abusers; they can't take so much as a Tylenol without the fear of falling back into the habit. As difficult as it may be for that drinker or drug user to develop and maintain a better and healthier life, all they really have to do is to never take that first drink or use that first drug. A lot of the other life altering habits we struggle with may be more difficult to beat. One thing is for sure, and that is it won't get better until we admit we have a problem.

Over the years, there has been much debate about alcoholism, as to whether it is a disease or simply a serious behavioral problem. Our government has won over and decided that by calling it a disease, at the very least, the responsibility of treating it could be transferred onto the backs of the public as well as the insurance companies, which since the enactment of the Affordable Health Care Act, are one and the same.

Similarly, many drug treatment programs now teach the drug user that it may not have been their fault that they are addicts, because it may just be in their genetics. If they can look back in their family history and see that Uncle Joe or Grandpa Claude drank too much or smoked weed during the days of Woodstock, then it must be in the family. The tendencies towards compulsive, addictive behavior must be in their blood, and of course, let's call it a disease, so it will be covered and the abusers won't feel so bad about themselves.

This is certainly not the beginning, but since about 2007, it has been stepped up big time, feeding the American people, "It's not your fault, someone else is responsible." "It's not your fault that you're poor or in debt, forget the fact that you've spent the last decade living and spending like a drunken sailor." "It's not fair that everyone doesn't make the same amount of money, forget the fact that everyone didn't earn it, and the fact that everyone didn't bother to make themselves more employable." "It's not your fault that your home is being foreclosed, forget the fact that you agreed to pay for it, and now decided not to do so. Forget the fact that you could have bought a smaller more affordable home, but instead chose to make the big gamble and go for it." "That didn't work out, so let's blame someone else."

Though not much has been done to fix the problem, it's been very obvious for some time that obesity and related conditions, such as diabetes and heart disease have grown to epic proportions in the past decades. So what does our government under the Obama administration choose to do? They absolve people (the voters) of all responsibility and tell them "It's not your fault." In 2013, at a time when we've never had so many overweight people, when it's estimated that nearly a third of our children and adolescents are not just a few pounds overweight but obese, and 30% of our children have cholesterol problems, they come out and tell us, "It's not your fault." "It's not your fault that your child is unhealthy nearly to a point of child abuse. It's not your fault that you have nearly fed your child to death. It's a disease, you're off the hook." And oh by the way, at the same time, this transfers all the responsibility over to the public. Yes, like everything else, we'll make the public pay for your sins, your laziness, and your ignorance. In 2013, the American Medical Association (AMA) came out and made a declaration that obesity is now a "multi-metabolic and hormonal disease." Now that this designation has been applied to a condition that up until recently was considered to be due to things such as poor eating habits and lack of exercise or activity, once again the American people can go about their day, blaming someone else; "**Poor me, I have a condition**."

There will be no more need for that New Year's resolution to lose weight and get in shape. It will simply be a time to update and make sure that your Obama Care policy is in place and that all of your dangerous lifestyle choices can be covered or fixed at someone else's expense. Eat up and sit around, after all, it's a disease.

Our president spent most of his life as a smoker, so of course any policy qualifying under Obama Care must cover tobacco counseling and remove any self-responsibility whatsoever from another self-destructive behavior. Thankfully, Mr. President, narcissism and neuroticism are and have been covered for some time, since they fall under mental illness. You see, at least these conditions are not self-inflicted but in many cases can leave a trail of devastating results to those around you. And just like the alcoholic, those afflicted with these conditions will rarely seek help until they have ruined many lives.

The bulk of the American people have been grouped together and told that they are the middle class, even though an overwhelming number of them were never or never should have been in this grouping, as they were only living "the life" on borrowed money and it was never real. Yet they were included because the more people that could be included in this group, the larger the group of voters, and what were these voters told? "It's not your fault," "The middle class is not being treated fairly," and "It's someone else's fault."

Unlike any time in history, in the last few years, an entire nation has been conditioned to believe that someone else is always responsible, that nothing is their fault, and that regardless of what they do or how they live their lives, they don't have to take responsibility. As a result, we've got a nation of self-indulgent, non-productive people acting strictly out of the desire for instant gratification with no thought about costs or consequences.

Millions of people have not gone to work for more than a year. Think of it, every morning for a year, other people get up, drive to work, and contribute to society. But these people, most of them the long-term unemployed, want to blame someone else. They've been told, "It's the economy." "The bankers did this." "The Democrats or the Republicans are at fault." Many of these people simply would not even consider a job that is less than what they once had, after all, that would be beneath them. Just who do these people think they are? Maybe if they weren't constantly being fed and financially supported, they would get off their lazy butts and start doing their part in rebuilding this nation.

EVEN TRUMAN BURBANK FINALLY FIGURES IT OUT

The Truman Show, starring Jim Carrey as Truman Burbank, was a hit movie in 1998. Truman lived until he was about 30 years old, content with what seemed to be a satisfying life, his every need always being met, and when anything did go slightly wrong, it seemed as if someone miraculously took care of it. He never stopped to question how or why things happened because he never had to.

His entire life was a reality show, none of it was real. From his birth and through the next thirty years, he was the subject of a TV show where, unbeknownst to him, the cameras were following him 24 hours per day and his life was being transmitted globally to every household around the world. Everyone, from his wife, friends, and even his father were actors, and each day was scripted for everyone else but Truman. He never questioned any of it since he had never known any different.

When things finally started to unravel, Truman set out to discover the truth. He initially thought his entire life was a figment of his imagination, but it turned out to be more like a puppet show, where he had been fed and led to react and act as expected by the directors of the show. The directors had fed him just enough satisfaction, as well as just enough fear of the outside in order to keep him where he was, doing what he had always done.

Thirty years, an entire lifetime, now how could a human being have lived that long being deceived and blind enough to believe the life he'd been living was real when it was completely false? Then again, if this could go on for thirty years, why couldn't it go for another thirty and yet another thirty? At the point where Truman finally got up enough curiosity and strength to not only discover the truth but to start taking some control of his own life, the producers were about to introduce the next generation of Trumans by having his (actress) wife have a baby, at which point the show would have evolved into a multi-generational sham.

The fact is that, though a massive big business entity had gone to great lengths to continue the farce for decades, it was simply not sustainable and inevitably the end had to come. And, of course, the longer the lies were told, the more creative the feeders had to get to keep up the deceit. Thirty years of scripting and re-scripting, all the time knowing that this couldn't end well. These guys continued year after year to deceive Truman and the rest of the world, partially because they didn't know how to end it. As expected, it eventually did come to an end, and Truman finally realized that everything he had been led to believe, every day of his life was not real. Though he had no way of knowing what to expect, he found a way to get out, to change his life and to break away from the feeders that he had become so dependent upon.

The Truman Show came out about the same time that our entire country had been going through a very similar scenario, with a large portion of the nation being appeased with free stuff, easy credit, welfare, government checks for sitting at home, lack of consequences or responsibility, and people were beginning to believe that everything they had been receiving was a right and that it would never end. But, just like anything that is not sustainable, our country had been in the middle of at least an attempted turn around. We had been going through a long process of welfare reform in an attempt to give the masses of people who had been living off others for so long, a deadline as well as assistance in getting off their dependency on government feeders and incentives, to at least begin to become more self-sufficient, and maybe even being contributors instead of takers. Following a couple of decades of faster growing deficits and a large national debt, we were finally to a point where we were actually balancing the federal budget, mainly due to the great ingenuity of our country's entrepreneurs and the resulting job growth. But just like anything that grows too fast, our economy, the stock market, and people's paltry 401(k) accounts ballooned, and people were feeling wealthy. Stock valuations swelled to extremes for any company with a dot-com behind their name, and all other company valuations followed. Home values were artificially inflated and people were borrowing money to invest in the ever-rising stock market. It seemed as if, overnight, every household in America had become middle class and they liked it. It was becoming so obvious that this was a "bubble" that just wasn't going to end well, so much that a person like Truman Burbank could have seen it. But people didn't want it to end, so they wouldn't admit that or believe that it was true. No one, from the politicians to the Fed wanted this thing to explode on their watch, so the feeding continued. The entire nation was living the life of Truman.

That's about the time when the craziness started getting kicked into high gear. Everything going forward from then until today, from continuously lowering interest rates to big business bailouts, with everything from sending checks in the mail to Americans to get them out and spending, to all the free stimulus programs, and then the mortgage forgiveness programs, all orchestrated in an effort to feed the American people enough to get them through the next election cycle and kick the can down the road.

We are now at a point where if the bulk of Americans weren't consumed every minute of their day and night with constant entertainment from reality shows, sports, and social media, if they would take just a few minutes and read the news and think for themselves, they would be unable to ignore the fact that the feeder trough is about to go dry. Life as they've known it, much like Truman, is about to change.

We've got what economists refer to as a "Demographic Cliff," with the largest group of Americans in history at or near retirement age, and the majority under the illusion that social security will somehow just be there, even though it is now obvious that it can be depended on about as much as a Bernard Madoff Ponzi account. Beyond the expected social security payments, at least a few are lucky enough to have the promise of at least some kind of company pension. Unfortunately, most of those are grossly underfunded and likely will not be there for long. A huge number of government employees are banking on public pensions, and we all know what kind of shape those are in. Plain and simple, the Boomers retirement accounts are so grossly underfunded that it is utterly ridiculous.

DON'T FEED THE SQUIRRELS

Add to that the new "Affordable Health Care" promises that are slated to be paid for with borrowed money, the millions of people expecting the promised Medicare and Medicaid coverage, and it all adds up to nothing short of the most massive entitlement crisis in history. The American people have intentionally been conditioned on a nearly daily basis to the word "crisis," to the point where the word is now largely ignored. People now hear these things so often that it simply goes in one ear and out the other.

Make no mistake, none of these things and none of these promises can be fulfilled. It is impossible and our government leaders know it, but as usual, they are hoping it can continue at least until they leave office. People, the time has come. We've got nearly 50 million people receiving food stamps, and every dollar is being borrowed, every day, day in and day out, yet people don't seem concerned. The number of households receiving food stamps increased by nearly one million between 2012 and 2013, nearly 1 in 5 households, at a time that was supposed to be an economic recovery. This is not getting better, and in fact every entitlement seems to be doled out lately as if there is no limit or no end.

The vast majority of people in the country don't trust the government, yet they seem to be content to be dependent on it. One thing that has become abundantly clear is that as long as there are squirrel feeders, there will be squirrels to feed, and the more feeders that are created, the more squirrels will become dependent on the feedings.

We've been brainwashed to put so much emphasis on higher education, at the same time as it has become so out of reach as far as affordability that it only exists thanks to free credit and more debt. The young people, at least the born-American Americans have been programmed to think that most jobs are beneath them. In fact, they are being encouraged and incentivized to spend nearly a third of what used to be their working years at home on Momma's couch and staying on Mom and Dad's healthcare plan until age 26. We "old guys" certainly can't expect to be taken care of if the young people aren't even entering the real life workforce until their thirties.

We've now got entire generations of people who put more thought and importance into their next tattoo than their waistline, and the same people are literally killing their own children through overfeeding, and keeping them uneducated. See any pattern here? Have the "Fed," become the "Feeders?"

Literally half the nation pays no federal income tax. The majority of the remaining people pay a fraction of their share of what it takes to run a nation like ours, even if it wasn't running up and paying for massive debt. The only ones left to pay the tax bill are the rich and those are the only job creators left.

It should be obvious to anyone that as soon as you get more than half the people getting a free ride, it will become nearly impossible to elect someone who tells them that "We can't continue to do that." As a result, our country with the great Democratic system elected a leader who promised everybody free stuff, convinced the bulk of the nation that they were entitled to everything from free food, no taxes, to free healthcare, and no one, at least none of that more than 50% cared to or thought to question this.

The entire nation has been conditioned like a hamster or cow to think that it's normal to buy anything and everything before you can afford it. People have gotten to a point where they swell their ego, not by what they own, but by what they have in their possession, as most people own very little. Sadly, these same people, whom their children have looked up to, are now no different than the adult squirrels that lived their entire lives not straying from the feeder, existing entirely off the Hoody's. So, what lesson are we now passing onto the little squirrels?

Today the majority of children are growing up like Truman, never experiencing or even witnessing reality. They think that food comes from a box and is paid for with a government coupon or card. They've never helped Dad fix the car because they've never had one that's without warranty. If these kids were to figure out how to go get a job when they're 16 or 18, they don't know which end of a shovel or rake to use since they've never done any manual labor. They've witnessed their parents more focused on their tattoos and personal appearances than whether they've stored away any nuts for the winter. They've learned that marriage, something that was once a lifetime contract, is today a more temporary agreement of convenience. Just like Wimpy, promising to gladly pay Tuesday for a hamburger today, instant gratification and selfish self-indulgence has been practiced and witnessed to a point of disgust. They've seen examples leading them to believe there are no negative consequences for bad decisions or bad deeds. Smoke and drink all you want and someone will be there to fix you with public supplied care. Lose your job and you'll continue to receive a check forever, buy more house than you can afford and Obama will be there to bail you out with more borrowed money. The bank is where you borrow, not where you save.

Probably the worst of examples of what we've taught to our children has occurred in the last 6 years. They may have gone to church on Sunday, but they've been told one thing and witnessed another. Back to, "Do as I say, not as I do." Wrath, Greed, Sloth, Pride, Lust, Envy, and Gluttony, which for centuries we've been told are bad things, are now coming from our leader, our own president. The "gimme" mentality, the "haves and have-nots," the hatred and envy towards anyone who works and saves to get ahead; we've gone one hundred years backwards when it comes to equality and acceptance, discrimination and hatred.

No, people, I may have fed the squirrels when I was young, and I even continued to teach or allow my children to feed the squirrels to a point where, at least in a couple localities, the squirrels may be extinct, but I didn't vote for Barack Obama and I'll do everything within my power to help to educate people and prepare people for the rude awakening when the feeder is ultimately taken away.

KEGGERS OR POTLUCKS

I remember as a child, every Halloween we would go trick-or-treating. There was never a purchased costume, so every year I was a bum, which basically consisted of putting on some old clothes that were too big for me. One year, like an idiot, I constructed a robot costume out of foil covered cardboard boxes. I netted about half the candy take that year and did nothing but slow the whole group down. We would go door to door, sometimes late into the evening, until finally the lights were all out and people were in bed. My candy carrier was a pillow case, partially because we would have never gotten any kind of store bought plastic pumpkin or container, and besides, we were putting in a full shift and any container we were heading out with was going to have to carry some loot. We started the minute it began to get dark, maybe about 5:00 pm and didn't quit until about 11:00 or so. Over time, we came to know which homes had the best candy—maybe even a full-sized candy bar—and we made sure to hit those houses. But there was always one house here and there that would either stiff the kids, or just as bad, give out, one little piece of hard candy. Of course, those houses that didn't give us "our fair share," were the ones that were sure to "get hit," hit with eggs, hit with soaped windows, you name it. Now, I'm not saying that I personally did or didn't participate in these actions, but one thing was for sure, those people who didn't contribute got the message. However, I don't know when it was, but at some point in my trick-or-treating years, I can remember doing the simple math to figure out how taking the time to soap those "blankety-blank" deadbeats' windows was measurable to the candy that would be lost, besides, why should I take the time to do it when someone else assuredly will?" I'm not sure that everyone had the system so calculated as we did. You know, take only the short driveways; forget the long ones. Always have one leader who stays half a house ahead of the group so as to handle ringing the doorbell so the rest of us could arrive just in time to grab a handful as the leader is already off to the next, leaving no lost time. But we were raised right and taught to be polite to adults, so when we ran to the steps, if the person told us to take just one, that's exactly what we did. But if they didn't say anything, heh, grab what you can, shout out "thank you!" and on to the next. And NEVER make eye contact, as that would only result in having to carry on a conversation that could cost 30 seconds or so. Oh, and yes we were the ones that didn't stop until the people finally had to ask us for ID, and say, "I think you're too old for this." Come to think of it, it was about the same time that I started carrying fake ID to buy beer, too old for candy and too young for beer, a real awkward age.

The reason I bring this up is that I can see now what I didn't realize then, in that as children, we just expected the candy to be there, no different than we expected dinner would be provided at home. We were there to take that candy, in fact we expected it to be there so much that we felt entitled, after all, it had always been there. Not only did we feel that we were entitled, we never stopped to think that we were giving nothing in return. At least when the three-year-old shows up at the door dressed in a cute little costume, the candy provider gets to enjoy the cute little kid, they may even get to talk to the child or parent and get a laugh or a smile, in which case each party is contributing something. Well, each one of us was once that three year old, but year after year, the longer the handouts were just there for the taking, it seemed the more we expected to receive and the less we provided back. Thank goodness that Halloween came just once a year. Even the squirrels could probably handle a once-a-year handout without getting hooked permanently and ruining their lives.

So, we hadn't learned much of a lesson from those childhood trick or treating handouts, except that nothing lasts forever and that at some point we were going to have to buy our own candy. So there we were, too old to get free candy and too young to even purchase beer.

I had a friend or two who were a little older than I was, so at the age of 14-15 or so, we were riding around in cars, drinking, and partying like there was no tomorrow. By 16 or 17, I was providing beer and other alcohol to my classmates on a regular basis, taking orders for Friday night, marking it up, and making a healthy profit. It was a regular business, just another example of supply and demand. I had one of the limited supplies and there seemed to be no limit on demand. Back then, in the early 70s, drinking and driving was a bad thing to do, we just didn't realize it, and it seemed that as a teenager, getting pulled over while drinking or even being smashed wasn't much of a big deal. The sheriff's deputies would usually just make us pour it out. As a result of there being virtually no consequences, drinking and driving around was what we did on a regular basis.

If it wasn't drinking parties with cases and cases of beer, it would be keg parties (keggers). There was always a kegger, and if not ours, then we knew where someone else's was. It could be at someone's house if their parents weren't home, or on the power line or at the river. It didn't take much planning, just get a keg or two, head out and crank up the music, and people showed up. It was common knowledge, at least to most, that as you showed up, you headed right to the organizer or host and tossed in a few bucks, sometimes more. Girls were never asked to pay (for obvious reasons), but if you showed up with a girl, you would contribute for two. The supplying of booze and the parties were separate, at least for me, as I never tried to make money on the parties, just simply to cover the overhead. Most of the kids that showed up didn't have quite as easy access to booze so they were very appreciative to be included and more than happy to contribute their fair share. But there seemed to always be some, and usually the same ones that showed up, drank someone else's booze and didn't pay a dime. It was only a matter of time until they would not only not be invited, but actually asked to leave.

Each of us grew up, and just like the trick-or-treating, we left the high school drinking parties behind us. It seems like in a flash, we each ended up where we are today. Over the years, we've all been to every imaginable gathering or outing, from picnics to family gatherings, camping to weddings, fundraisers to funerals, and we've all eaten the food, ridden on the boats, and listened to the music. We've dirtied the dishes, blown off the fireworks, drank the wine, and pooped in the toilet.

DON'T FEED THE SQUIRRELS

How about the potluck gatherings where everyone is expected to bring something, some may bring a potato salad, another fried chicken, or maybe paper plates and forks, soft drinks, or a bottle of wine. There is always someone who shows up with nothing, another who always goes the extra mile with all sorts of homemade goodies, or the person who swings by the deli and grabs something quick. I've noticed that it is always the same people who conveniently leave just before cleanup time, never offering to help, and leave someone else with a sink full of dirty dishes, piles of garbage, and the mess. These are the same people who are happy to leave with much more than they arrived with.

My daughter is amazing in the kitchen. She always seems to show up at the kids' events with very creative and unique cookies, or dishes that she obviously put a lot of effort and thought into. She's very good at that type of thing, both the creativity and thoughtfulness. Not everyone is as good in the kitchen as she is, and frankly, it's probably preferred if that person swings by and buys a dozen cookies from the bakery, or shows up with chips or soft drinks. What really counts is that each person contributes what they can.

I can remember as a child, every Christmas Eve we were able to open one gift that night and the rest would be under the tree, from Santa, but in addition we opened relatives' gifts from those that were celebrating with us. It seemed like forever, but we would wait either for my dad to come home from work or for Grandpa and Grandma. Dad was never much of a drinker, but it seemed that he and his co-workers always chose that night after work to stop off for a couple of celebratory drinks. Even so, he usually would still get home before Grandpa and Grandma (my mom's parents). I'll always remember the huge grin on Grandpa's face as he came walking in carrying huge boxes of beautifully wrapped gifts. His big smile was undoubtedly partially due to a few holiday cheers himself, along with the fact that he was happy to bring all of us kids these gifts. What he didn't know, and I'm sure nobody ever let on, was that Grandma was a lousy gift giver. We learned that early on and we were always ready to smile, say thank you, and quickly move on. Grandma bought everything from a catalog, and she always bought in bulk. It was not unusual for me to receive the same green plaid shirt three years in a row, or the exact model car or airplane as the year before. And you could be sure that the cousins would show up in a green plaid shirt and have the same model on their shelf. She may have rarely got it right with gift giving, but she never showed up empty handed. You can bet that she did the best she could. She never showed at a family gathering without some dish, homemade something, which was usually unrecognizable to us kids, and sadly rarely eaten, but she always contributed what she could. Though, back in those days, unlike today, it was rare when anyone didn't at least try to contribute their share or more, but even then, I can think of at least one relative that always showed up empty-handed and left with all the leftovers after drinking everyone else's drinks and without even an offer to lift a finger to clean up.

Today, there are many more than that one relative. We've got half the nation that pays absolutely no income tax. They're showing up at the party every day, empty-handed, just to leave, every day, with armloads of handouts. Can you blame the rest of us for not being too happy to see these party crashers drive up? And then of course, there are the ones that host every event, provide most of the stuff, and are left to clean up the mess, and then every person in between, the ones who contribute something but nowhere near their fair share. That's like arriving with a bag of potato chips and leaving with a trunkful of meat, pie, and booze.

It's the same at every party, at every event, every day. The same people contribute nothing and take the most. There are many who do the minimum and expect the maximum, and then the one-percenters. My grandma is excused because she did the very best she could, and if she was alive today I would be happy to invite her every day, as I'm sure she would have Grandpa loaded down. In fact, anyone in this country who is willing to do the best that they can, well, they're invited to my party anytime, and as far as the rest of the deadbeats that continue to receive and rarely if ever give, well they might as well be back soaping those windows.

DON'T FEED THE SQUIRRELS

IS GOOD EVEN GOOD ENOUGH?

As I'm deep into the writing of this book, I have become more and more conscious of the fact that a reader may by this time begin to think, 'Just who in the heck does this guy think he is?' Do I come off too condescending, as if patronizing the readers, when in reality I'm probably as guilty, or guiltier than most, of life's mistakes or wrong roads, as illustrated in my writings? By this time, I'm thinking to myself that I've probably ticked off and possibly alienated pretty much everybody, including my close friends and relatives, when all I set out to do was one, vent my frustrations, and two, hopefully help others improve their future by learning not only from my own mistakes but from years of observations.

So, I went to my office on a Sunday morning in June, which coincidentally happened to be Father's Day. Before I entered, I looked through the glass door and saw on the floor, scattered around, numerous envelopes that had been shoved through the mail slot. I knew these were rent checks, as we own and manage a large number of rental homes and many people drive and deposit their rent money on the day it is due. This being the 15th of the month, there was only a half dozen or so checks, whereas around the 1st or 2nd of each month I might arrive at the office on a weekend like this and see a pile of thirty or forty envelopes where people had made delivery at the last minute. Frankly, walking up on a Saturday or Sunday morning and seeing that huge pile of checks on the floor of our office is kind of fun and gives me a good feeling that maybe the last 30 or so years of building and accumulating properties was somehow worth it.

But this morning as I entered I found something other than the usual rent payments. There on the floor was a paperback book, and at first glance it had kind of a religious appearance. Tucked inside was a small typewritten note from the pastor of the church down the street, but it was not addressed to anyone specifically. Though it may have been intended for any one of a dozen people in our office, due to recent happenings in my life, I had to question whether maybe this was intended for me. Normally I would see something like this, shove it aside, and go on with my busy day, but after skimming through the first few pages, I was hooked, as this particular book had special meaning to me. So, for the next couple of hours, any of the things that I had planned to work on were set aside as I sat and read this little book cover to cover.

Both as a disclaimer as well as a promotion, I'd like to dedicate this entire chapter of my book to the author of the small life-changing book, and in doing so, recommend that everyone, whether religiously inclined or not, pick up this book and do as I did, put things aside for two hours and read it.

The book I'm recommending is **How Good is Good Enough? by Andy Stanley**. It's less than 100 pages and is certainly worthwhile.

Throughout this chapter I may copy or quote word for word from Mr. Stanley's book, or blend in some thoughts with my own.

I was intrigued as to how much, at least in my thinking, his book paralleled mine, except with a completely different twist. His book focuses more on helping readers put thought into religious beliefs, trying to decipher who will and how to live for eternity, and what it may take to enter Heaven, whereas my book is merely attempting to get each of us successfully through the rest of life on this side of the grave. Both of our books try to help people realize just how little thought they are probably putting into both the rest of this life and the time beyond and how most or nearly all of us expect that everything will be alright.

I'll start out with relaying word for word, a story that begins on the first page of Stanley's book. The story goes like this:

A Sunday school teacher was to explain to the six-year-olds in his class what someone had to do in order to go to Heaven. In an attempt to discover what the kids already believed about the subject, he asked a few questions.

"If I sold my house and my car, had a big garage sale, and gave all my money to the church, would that get me into Heaven?" "No!" the children all answered.

"If I cleaned the church every day, mowed the yard, and kept everything neat and tidy, would that get me into Heaven?" Again the answer was, "NO!"

"Well then," he said, "If I was kind to animals and gave candy to all the children and loved my wife, would that get me into heaven?" Again they all shouted, "NO!"

"Well then, how can I get into heaven?" A boy in the back row stood up and shouted, "YOU GOTTA BE DEAD!"

The author went on to explain, as most would agree, that death is a prerequisite. That is about the extent of where any sort of agreement ends and where speculation begins. The majority of his book is predicated on the idea that most people want to believe that good people go to Heaven, and as long as they live their lives doing more good than bad, they're a shoe-in for entry through the pearly gates. This small book is able to explain that this popular way of thinking is based on a theory that makes no sense at all, but intelligent people continue to believe mainly because it is the easiest thing to do.

Earlier in my book I brought up the idea that we may be judged on a curve when being sorted for entry or denial into Heaven. His views seem to go along the same lines, except to point out the absurd silliness of the belief that all it takes to get into Heaven is being good. Even though humans' mortality rate is 100%, and no one has any idea of whether they have fifty years or fifty minutes left, everyone seems to think that there is plenty of time left to stash away enough good deeds to counterbalance their bad ones.

The author points out that most people choose a religion like they're choosing a flavor of ice cream. They pick what they like by what suits their taste at that particular time and what they feel comfortable with, and then what's worse, they, or we, tend to dissect it and believe and or implement only the parts that work for us, and of course with the least effort. That makes us feel good, as though now we're covered, we're doing mostly good stuff, so everything from here on out that happens to us will be good.

People pay attention only to what they want to hear at church or in the rest of their lives. Any person with even half a brain, anyone who owns a television, radio, or has ever picked up a newspaper should not be able to avoid the obvious, the iron-clad evidence, essentially the "gospel," that the life they have been living cannot and will not continue, but somehow in the back of their minds, everything will be OK. The other author's book speaks similarly to how few people believe that they won't be going to a good place after death, even though they've put virtually no effort into the assurance of that. He points out that almost 90% of people surveyed believed there is a Heaven, while only 30% believed in Hell, and almost nobody who believed in Hell thought they were going there.

If you believe the Bible to be true and you remember the story of Adam and Eve, one could be very irritated by the fact that we and all mankind are paying for their poor choices. I find it so ironic that some things never change, whether we refer to there always being a tipping point or that the pendulum will always swing too far in one direction before it goes too far in the other direction. Stanley's book looks at Biblical times to the unknown eternity, while this book you're reading is limited mostly to a few generations. Similar to others eternally having to pay for Adam and Eve's sins or poor choices, the people of our nation, both today and in the coming decades or possibly centuries will be paying a heavy price for all of the selfish actions of the most recent decades.

In the grand scheme of history, our great country is very young. It's been in existence for a very short time, but for the first 200 years people were pretty self-reliant and responsible, and for the most part, with a few exceptions, were able to hand off the country to the next generation in better shape than they inherited it. It's been mostly in the last 35-40 years, the very time when most or all of us shared the responsibility, that we selfishly plucked the apple off the tree, and now it may be too late to put it back.

FEEDING THE TERRORISTS

So many times I've seen the squirrels at parks or busy camp grounds running and playing, jumping from branch to branch as if they hadn't a care in the world. The truth is this particular group of critters probably didn't have a care in the world, since they can play while tourists continue to feed them. They laugh at us, thinking, 'Stupid humans, working all week, just to come out here and spend your money on free handouts for us.'

Now, imagine if these cute little creatures were enormous in size, nasty in demeanor, and would just as soon bite your head off than look at you. Would it be smart to feed them? Would it be cute?

Every day I see the news on the television, or a picture in the newspaper of large groups of frightening-looking men screaming out horrific, bloodcurdling screams, and almost always pointing an assault rifle above their heads. The first thing I think is, 'Where did those weapons come from?' They're usually piled in the back of a Ford truck, an armored Humvee, or some other U.S.-made military type vehicle. These crazed looking militants are almost always armed to the hilt, looking to kill the very people who supplied them with everything, from the clothes they're wearing to the vehicle they are being transported in, you might say the very hand that fed them; the Americans. These people, hundreds of thousands of these people are vicious, blood-thirsty murderous killers with nothing else in their lives except the desire to kill everyone in the world that doesn't share in their beliefs. And our leaders, yes, our very own American leaders supplied and continue to supply them, as if they were a bunch of cute little creatures next to the park bench, except instead of Hoody's, we're giving them the very tools needed to destroy us and our freedom.

Day after day, year after year, we continue to feed them with everything from helicopters to rifles and ammunition, armored Humvees to tanks and rockets. Then, what is just plain sickening and embarrassing is the way the American people act about violence. Maybe we hear of a drive-by shooting, or a lone gunman going on a shooting spree in a shopping mall or public center, and immediately the spineless, ignorant, vulnerable citizens here at home will go on an anti-gun campaign, buying back guns and destroying them, limiting access to them, and doing everything within their power to outlaw guns or any other form of personal protection. The American people have been taken care of and babied for so long, conditioned to think that they will always be taken care of with zero thought of the bully down the street, the murderous killer loose in the neighborhood, or what's most likely to take us out, the enormous armies of militant extremists with only one thing on their minds; an absolute hatred for Americans. These armies of crazies, armed with an immense quantity of U.S. armaments, are one plane ride or boat ride away. They have passports and they can come and go as they please. Heck, many of them have been previously apprehended as terrorist suspects and released to kill again.

This president, Mr. Obama is right when he continues to point out that he didn't get us into these wars in Iraq and Afghanistan, but he took on the job of Commander in Chief, so it's just not right for him to take the next eight years off and pretend that the turmoil on the other side of our world doesn't exist. For years we've been blindly sending weapons and wealth all over the globe, trying to pick the least bad "Bad Guy" to back. When we're done with these "allies," we turn them away, giving little thought to what we may have caused. The people in this country think that if we take the guns off our streets and out of our homes, it will solve all our problems and eliminate violent crimes in one of the most civilized countries in the world. Then we close our eyes to the spreading of weapons around as if we were using a manure spreader in some of the most volatile, violent places in the world, allowing them to get in the hands of the absolute most dangerous people alive today.

Saddam Hussein was a bad guy, but he was probably one of the best bad guys around when it came to keeping some type of order in the Middle East. As far as dictators go, he was probably one of the best, if there is such a thing. Between Daddy Bush and Baby Bush, they did a tremendous job of showing the world the enormous might and military capabilities of the U.S. In doing so, they assured decades of revenue streams, in the trillions of dollars, of borrowed U.S. money to their friends and supporters, the arms dealers, oil companies, etc. They also set us on a course of bankrupting our great country, and the ultimate demise of thousands of American lives as well as setting the world up for possibly the next world war or, at the very least, stirring up a bee hive in the Middle East that may never be tamed back down. Then, at a time when we are in need of a leader more than ever before, Barack Obama tells a bunch of lies and makes enough empty promises to the growing group of ignorant voters, that he gets himself elected as our president and immediately decides to take the next eight years off and go golfing or do interviews and press releases. Seriously, if we could just pay this guy to stay home and hire one of those "Highly-paid CEOs" that he keeps putting down, to lead this country, maybe, just maybe we could still save this country, and the lives as well as way of life that we all just expect will still be here tomorrow.

Osama bin Laden, Ibrhim Ibn Awwad, Ibn Ibrahim, Ali Ibn Muhammad as-Badri al-Hashimi-Husayni, al-Qurashi (aka) Caliph Ibrahim, ISIS, Jihadist militants, Sunni militants, Islamic extremists, Al-Qaida, insurgents, Sunni Arab extremists, Jihadist groups, Jihadist cause, who is the flavor of the month? You may as well be at Baskin and Robbins picking from 31 flavors of ice cream when picking who we should supply with weapons and pallet loads of our borrowed United States currency.

The U.S. seems to always think we know better than the rest of the world about people whom we actually know very little about. So we pick the "Bad Guy" who we think is the least bad "Bad Guy," and shower them with a steady stream of weapons and supplies, enough to outfit an army just to later find that maybe we backed the wrong "Bad Guy," or that the "Bad Guy" we backed and supplied laid down his arms and ran, leaving enough arms and ammunition to supply hundreds of thousands of worse "Bad Guy" fighters for years.

Like bread crumbs being spread around on the ground in the park to feed the animals, we've been spreading major weapons around the world, invoking chaos and brutality. We then sit back and wait and as these crazies fight amongst themselves, inevitably getting to a point where we Americans can't stomach it, and our answer is always to go back and feed them more.

Just how is it that we are so gullible to think that it makes sense to pay to do "gun buy-backs" to get a few guns off the streets here in the most civilized nation in the entire world, and then spread the most lethal weaponry around to the most violent neighborhoods of the world. This type of unforgivable activity benefits only the arms manufacturers, the private military contractors, and the politicians on the receiving end of their support.

An individual citizen in this country can be imprisoned for forgetting to lock the gate to their back yard swimming pool, improperly strapping their child into a car seat, or leaving their personal weapon unlocked in their own home in the event that harm should come to someone due to their negligence. But, as a nation, we think nothing of spreading weaponry around the globe without even so much as a warning label. People, we're not feeding a bunch of squirrels here, no, we're feeding an enormous population of ferocious animals who will undoubtedly want more.

What most Americans just can't seem to accept or understand is that every penny of the billions of dollars being spent to keep the world fed with these weapons is being borrowed, contributing to the bankruptcy of our once-great nation. A strong nation is a wealthy nation, and each day, whether borrowing more money to send weapons to the crazies who want to kill us or giving pizzas to the Hoggy Hogs to buy votes for self-serving un-patriotic politicians, our country continues to get weaker and broker. What do you suppose happens when the feed runs out?

PARENTS, SHAME ON YOU

As parents, it's natural to want each of our children to be the best looking, smartest, and of course the star of each and every sport. But then, God forbid, if one should be born and by age 6, 10, or 12, be a little too short or tall, freckled faced, or in any way not quite like the rest, maybe taking 3 months longer to walk than the neighbor kid, or maybe he or she requires some extra classes or tutoring for speech or math. As parents, our heart pours out for them, as no one wants to see their child feel inadequate or be ridiculed by others. We even blame ourselves, since after all they are a combined creation of our self and our chosen mate. What happens when your teenage son comes to you and says, "Dad, why couldn't I be six-foot tall like my friend, Jimmy?" "Well, son, as you can see, I'm 5'-9' and your mother is 5'-2" (and a half). What do you think? Do you think you would rather be Jimmy?" The truth is, that 5'-8" kid is smarter, wittier, and much better looking than Jimmy, though he could never dunk the basketball; but probably because he couldn't dunk the ball, he quickly learned to handle the ball and move it up court like nobody else. And for rebounds, not being able to tower over the others, he learned to anticipate where the ball was going to be, an attribute that serves him well now in business and life. As for Jimmy's parents, yes they were taller than his mother and me. "Son, why do you think that it's rarely the lead horse that is first to come across the finish line?"

Keep them fed and housed, provide them with books and toys that will help them learn, and most importantly, provide a good example because, believe me, they are watching and listening. Beyond that, frankly, nearly every one of us has been doing our kids a disservice by giving them too much. We want them to have more or have it easier than we did. I thought we loved them; why are we idiots? We seemed to have gotten by just fine and looking back, I find that it wasn't what I got, but what I didn't get that drove me to go out and get it. I get together with my brothers and sister and we reminisce about the old days and our parents' parenting, saying things like, "What were they thinking about?" I'm ashamed to say it, but it really wasn't until I was sitting down writing this book that I came to the realization that my parents may have been a couple of the best parents in history. There were plenty of times, way into my adult life, that I felt shorted, maybe even gipped, and now it's too late to tell them, **"Thanks Mom and Dad for what you didn't do," since as it turns out, they did everything they needed to**. I would also want to give them a "Special thanks for not doing too much." I'm sure a lot of what they did by not doing, they never knew. It seems that, unbeknownst to me, some of it must have rubbed off on me and, luckily for me, I partnered up with a life partner with most of the same "give them just what they need" views. Though we assuredly did and gave more to our children, probably because we could, they grew up with wants but very few needs, and at an early age, unlike the little birdies, they weren't kicked out of the nest but were itching to get out on their own and fly. Now as they are watching their own children grow and mature, I'm seeing a lot of the same and feel very confident that our parents would be pretty darned proud to see what amazing grandparents and great-grandparents they turned out to be, to a big batch of smart, productive, and soon-to-be contributing children, many of whom they never had the opportunity to meet. It's too bad, but maybe not getting thanks till years after you're gone is just part of being a good parent.

Earlier in my building career I would do all of the homeowner orientation walk-throughs before buyers took possession of their new home. It was quite common that the buyers would bring along their parents. It was so common that I quickly learned that it was important to provide little features, materials or practices that the older people would recognize and associate with quality, such as wood wrapped windows or enclosed kitchen soffits, things that would remind them of the way homes used to be built. It wasn't enough to please the wife with the kitchen and master bath or the husband with the garage and extra parking for toys, because in many cases, if they were to have to come up with any down payment or closing costs, it was quite common that the parents were "helping them out." The story was always the same, just the faces and the car models changed. The parents would tell me, "**It's so tough for kids these days**," and then go on to tell me how they were helping them out. What's funny is that the "kids" drove up in separate vehicles, both late models, maybe a Jeep Cherokee and a BMW, or a jacked up four-wheel drive pick-up, while the parents' car was a 15-year-old sedan. And the house, well it certainly wasn't the family home like the one they grew up in. No, I'm pretty sure Mom and Dad's house didn't have a 3 or 4 car garage, a master bath the size of the kitchen, or for that matter a kitchen the size of a living room. The kids' new home would have more toilets than the parents had bedrooms. Bad, bad parents, I'm sure they meant well, but even more than the obvious that they were continuing to "feed" these adults as if they were still toddlers, they also assisted and enabled this unfortunate couple to get into something that they could no way in heck be able to afford or maintain; "Fly Birdie Fly." When I refer to this couple as "unfortunate," I really think they'd have been better off and had a better chance in life if they been orphans.

When my daughter and son were graduating from high school, only about 15 years ago, the cost of in-state college tuition was not nearly as expensive as it is today, and thankfully by that time in our lives, we could afford it. Both Erin and I, neither of us having had the opportunity at their age, were ecstatic that our children were able to go off and get that experience. We put no expectations on them except to say that we'd like to see them stick it out for at least one year, if for no other reason but to experience college and get out of town. But make no mistake, we took the expense pretty seriously and like anything else, hoped to get our money's worth. So you can imagine my concern when part way through my daughter's freshman year at a family gathering, her aunt, my sister asked her, "How do you like college?" Her face lit up with a big mischievous smile as she said, "I'm having the most fun I've ever had in my life." Well, that's not exactly what a father wants to hear from the innocent little girl that just left the nest, or is it? After a little thought, I looked at it just like her skinning her knee, having complete confidence that she was capable of making all the right decisions. I thought 'Honey, have all the fun you can, just be smart and safe.' Before we knew it she had her 4-year degree in less than 4-years and a job teaching two states and over 800 miles away. My son, being 3-years younger, also attended college in state. In fact, after his freshman year in a dorm room, he moved in and shared a little house that we had been renting out in his college town. After a couple of late night calls about eighty cars lined up and down the street and constant parties going on, we had reason for concern, but no less than his sister, he had our complete confidence and he did not disappoint us. From the day each of them left for college, it was like they left the gate running, but the fact is, they were working before and throughout college, getting more knowledge and just kept on going. I think we got our money's worth.

But that's just not the case in many, if not most families these days. For one, I hear a lot of parents telling the kids that they have to get a college degree or they'll never amount to anything. Well, that's just not the case, and frankly a good share of the high school graduates these days just aren't college material, or at the very least, they're not mature enough or emotionally ready, especially if you have any expectation of getting your money's worth.

First of all, are you kidding me? We can't educate a child in 13 years? From kindergarten to reading, writing, and arithmetic, most of the basics can be taught by the 6th grade, at least to a point where a person could get through a day in this country, reading road signs, earning and purchasing a loaf of bread, and typing a basic text into their iPhone. Could we and should we be able to accomplish this? I think so. Then we've got an additional six years, through high school graduation, in which to prepare these birdies to fly. And in many cases, ready or not, they're kicked out of the nest, expected that they know how to fly. Others will remain in the nest for another 10 or 12 years under Mommy and Daddy's wing, whether that be still at home or hiding out in the college babysitting system, in which case they come out into the real world already 1/3 of their way to death, ready to begin life, something many of their childhood friends have been experiencing for a decade.

Many kids are told by their parents that they need a college degree in order to get a job and the longer that they stay in the academic system instead of out experiencing life, that's exactly the best they can hope for, a job. Not that there is anything wrong with a job, but the point is that the job they get will likely be working for one of their past classmates who jumped into life years earlier.

Studies have shown that some higher education likely will enhance a young person's lifetime earning capabilities, but studies also show that the majority of degrees earned are not required or in many cases even relative to the position a person ends up in. Aside from the careers that require a specific degree or lengthy training, such as a doctor or lawyer, in most cases, the longer a person stretches out their time in college rather than out in the active workforce, the farther behind they will find themselves when compared to the early bloomers.

There is, without a doubt, a vast difference both academically and socially in each high school graduate, whether comparing students from different schools or geographical areas or even within the same classroom. The quality and diversity of the education will vary from school to school, as well as from one instructor to another, but the biggest difference in the level of readiness for society of each student stems from what they have or haven't learned outside of the classroom.

More than any time in the past, we hear and read of parents complaining that it is the job of the teachers to teach their kids, when at the same time we hear the teachers asking, "Where are the parents?" Both are right. First the teachers have a nearly impossible task in the few hours that they have the children if the parents aren't supportive and contributing, and even more importantly capable. The public school system requires school to be in session approximately 180 days per year, many of which end up being partial days, workshops, parent teacher conferences etc. Some days will get cut short for snow, others for holidays, etc. Then, to make it worse, the individual child can be absent a significant number of days due to illness or even a family trip to Disneyland and still be passed on to the next grade level. In the real world, this would be considered even less than part time.

My daughter had what my wife and I considered to be a lousy third grade teacher, but fortunately some of her other teachers more than made up for that lost and wasted time. Not only that, the very fact that the school day and school year is so short, her exposure to that sub-par teacher was minimal, leaving the overwhelming number of leftover hours in that year of her life and what she learned, up to us, the parents. But Brandi was lucky as, at least in my opinion, her mother and I collectively are at least average or better than average parents when it comes to our parenting and teaching abilities, as well as by being strong role models. So, even if we scored only average, only 50%, that would mean that there are at least half the families out there that are less, and many times much less qualified, to be teaching their children. And if that could be only for the third grade, maybe, just maybe those children could make up for lost time and opportunities in the remaining twelve years. But unfortunately for them, they'll be stuck with the same bad teachers each day when school lets out, every weekend, every holiday, all summer long, from the time they're born until they finally get away. Could it be that when a child drops out of school before graduating high school that it is no fault of the school system at school but more likely what they experience after school lets out?

We know that many times students are graded on a curve, and certainly if we look back on all the years and our children's teachers, we can judge them kindergarten through twelfth grade, the best, worst, and those in between, grading them 1 through 13. Well, the same goes for parents, the people that spend the most time with their child. In a classroom with thirty students, there will always be one child with the best parents, one child with the worst parents, generally those that spend the least time and have the weakest students, and the rest will fall somewhere in between. I can't guarantee it, but my guess is that when a child excels or bombs in their educational career, it is not due to their 3rd grade teacher.

So, how many parents encouraged their child to go out and take out a loan to go to college? The truth is the majority of parents that did are the same ones that themselves continue to sign onto a new seven-year auto loan every three years without really understanding or even reading what they're signing. Sound familiar? Most parents don't fully understand the difference between a grant and a loan, or a federally insured student loan from a private student loan, and many have never read the forms or promises that their children have signed. And just as I stressed earlier in the book, if you are buying a car now with the promise of paying for it later, then you can't afford that car. Many still hold onto the thought that they make x-amount per year, so they can easily afford the payment. Now, even with that flawed thinking, **if your child makes zero per year and you're encouraging them to go into debt for something with the promise of paying for it at a later date, maybe you should question if it's not time for your child to start listening to a different teacher.**

Seriously parents, if your grade on that curve isn't the number 1, top of the list, and for that matter, even if it is, get those kids out there working, out there experiencing something different, out there using a tool and taking direction, out there thinking for themselves, instead of watching and repeating your mistakes and living your life over.

DON'T FEED THE SQUIRRELS

WHAT HAVE WE LEARNED?

Squirrels will not police themselves. They really are not capable of saying "no" when offered a handout, and why would they when it seems so easy, and especially when they watch the others hogging down. And why would we expect humans to be any different? Put something in front of them and they're going to take it.

Early on I expressed my concern and guilt at how my family and I were participants in possibly causing the extinction of a group of squirrels at that scenic spot on top of a mountain pass. Then there was my brother on his acreage estate where, for years, he'd provided the squirrels with Hoody's, getting them hooked on the handouts just to one day wake up and realize the negative affect and near annihilation of another grouping of the innocent creatures. But if it were just the small number of critters that were wiped out, I would probably not give it another thought. No, messing with those squirrels had an effect on all the creatures around them, and there's really no way of knowing the damage done or time it may have taken for nature to restore things in those tiny isolated locations.

Thankfully in each of these instances, we're talking about such a tiny number of critters when you consider the hundred billion or so in the United States alone. So, our messing with nature and wiping out the squirrels probably isn't going to destroy the eco-system any more than you driving your automobile to work tomorrow morning is destroying life. With that being said, I certainly wouldn't go out and repeat that awful mistake every day, day in and day out, the feeding and decimation of the squirrel species that is.

The fact is, we could add up our and every other family's feeding of the squirrels across the nation and it would only affect a minute fraction of the population of squirrels. Unfortunately, when it comes to feeding of the humans, that's not the case. There would be no reason for concern with the American citizens being fed handouts, essentially Hoody's, if it were on the same scale of the squirrels, say less than 1%. The fact is, back to about 1940 and earlier, handouts and social services programs were there strictly for those in need, and probably in short supply and under-provided. It wasn't until maybe the late 1960s that our country really started to develop programs and some sort of organized method of providing assistance. Very quickly though, we went from a time when handouts were being given to about a tenth of one percent, meaning one in every thousand people, to today when nearly every person in our country has eaten the Hoody. That's right, nearly 100% of the people in our nation, including myself, my wife, children, and grandchildren have at least sampled the Hoody, and boy, once you've tried it, it's tough to get off of. If the squirrels were to be fed like the American people, they'd have been wiped out in no time, because just like the American people, they thought it would last forever. They never questioned where it was coming from because, 'hey, this is the way it always is.' But you know, the squirrels' feedings, their handouts, would've ceased when the Hoody's ran out.

Our nation has always been a nation of givers, too bad we've been made into a nation of takers. If my neighbor is hungry and I've got extra bread, you can bet I'll be there to help him out, assuming I've got enough bread to provide for my own family first. However, I'm not sure that I would go down to the bank and borrow money to buy bread to feed my neighbor. With a few exceptions, I think most people would do and act the same. It wasn't until the recent decades that our government has embarked on "bread for everyone," regardless of if we have any bread to give, "No worries, we'll borrow it." And borrow they did.

When the adult squirrel got the first handout from a traveling tourist on that mountain pass, it probably seemed so innocent and like some kind of windfall, and then every potato chip and Hoody thereafter made that squirrel less and less self-reliant. But then came the baby squirrels, always looking up, admiring and mimicking the adults, gorging on those Hoody's and other handouts as if they were a right, not a windfall, and never imagining that this fantasy life was not sustainable. Well, you know the story, but the difference in these squirrels and the people is that they don't vote. Every person in office wants to make it to the end of their term without everything falling apart, so they kick the can down the road. Contrary to many beliefs, the majority of our politicians are not idiots. In fact, when it comes to intelligence, they for the most part are in the top tier when compared with the general population, and most of them know that what they've been doing is crazy and destined for complete collapse, but just like the guy before them, the thinking is, 'not on my watch,' so they keep borrowing and filling the troughs with Hoody's. Scumbags! **They all ought to be locked up for treason for the damage they have done and are doing to our great country.**

As a Baby Boomer, I'm disgustingly ashamed to be part of this generation that not only allowed but participated in the destruction of a once great nation. But that doesn't mean I won't continue to take advantage of every ridiculous freebie handed out and available to every person, rich, poor and everywhere in between.

Any sane, reasonably intelligent, patriotic person might be thinking, 'but what can I do?' Well, to begin, if each one of us would simply wake up and realize just what a ridiculous point things have gotten to in this country, but more importantly, admit at least to ourselves that we've each fallen prey to the system and contributed to the problem, that would be a start. Then, just like the alcoholic, admitting it to ourselves will undoubtedly not stop us from continuing down this destructive path, since, just like that alcoholic, we still want that drink. This won't be easy, but each person individually has to realize that they have to stand up and admit "I ate the Hoody. I've been taking more than giving and I want to stop." I guess I'm dreaming if I actually think the majority of people are going to do this on their own, stop taking the handouts, start planning for tomorrow, and not depending on someone else to provide for their future.

What would happen if everyone all at once were to get responsible and stop, just immediately stop buying things that they can't afford? I'm not talking about whether you could afford a payment, but could afford to buy. Simply put, anything other than a home, and a home is another subject for discussion, anyone buying a car and not paying for it, can't afford it, plain and simple. **If you are considering the purchase of a car and you haven't saved the cash to purchase it, you cannot afford it. Without exception, any consumer item you purchase with the promise to pay later, be it an auto or a couch, an outfit or a meal, greatly reduces your ability to purchase anything, even food tomorrow and in many cases for years to come.** The system has been set up to feed us this free credit, and we have eaten it up. We may as well have been snorting cocaine up our nose or sticking a needle in our arm. Once hooked, it's hard to get off, short of going cold turkey. Our government and the system need transactions to happen in order to survive. Each time an auto or a couch is purchased taxes are assessed and spread around from federal, state to local taxing authorities, so it benefits the system to keep us spending. Spending is OK, but spending tomorrow's earnings is not, since it only takes a short time before this behavior is unsustainable and a person is working only to pay for yesterday's purchases, leaving them dependent on credit and debt today just to survive until tomorrow. It's a simple example of bad habits versus good habits, drug addicted versus clean living, self-reliant versus dependent addict. The short-term thinking on the part of our leaders is focused only on keeping us spending and nothing more, no vision or concern about what happens even next year or the year after. As the majority of people reading this view themselves to be self-reliant contributing citizens, they may scoff at these accusations of them or you, if you are in this same class or group of people who are or are about to be drags on society.

There is a reason why half of the people in this country don't pay Federal Income Tax. Because the system works better, at least today, if these people, many of you, have every penny in your pocket to go out and spend on consumer items and continue to make payments on yesterday's purchases and to go out and continue that craziness. After all, our government, at least for the short term, can make up for you not contributing your fair share of taxes to keep them afloat by simply creating more debt. It works for a while, it has worked up until now, but it has never worked in any other civilization for very long and we're about done. And every time the spending begins to falter, they have simply come up with lower interest rates, easier, lower or zero down payment programs. In some cases, they've gone as far as even sending a check to the majority of people just to get more money into the system and flowing, while at the same time driving up more debt, creating an even bigger bubble. So if everyone were to get responsible at the same time and just stop buying until they could afford it, it would be disastrous, or at the very least, very difficult for a while, for a long while, much like any other addict getting off heroin or any other addictive substance. But that's probably not going to happen since the system is surely going to continue to keep the feeding tube going as long as there are takers.

Think about yourself, just yourself and forget about everyone else. Like a classroom teacher grading on a curve, the more people around you that continue to live their lives in a counterproductive manner, the easier it will be for you to rise above and shine. If three years from now, you and your family were to find yourselves debt free, as opposed to where you are likely to be if you continue down this same road, and then you look at the poor fools who never made the change or couldn't break the bad habits, how will that make you feel? Imagine how you'll feel when you go to purchase that next new car, peel off the cash, and drive it home knowing that it's yours, and then the first of the next month, put the cash away in a drawer or better yet an income-producing investment that would have typically gone to pay interest on that depreciating old car, knowing that you'll be able to replace your car every few years for the rest of your life and never have a payment. You'll be sitting in that car dealership saying "No" to financing and extended warranties, all the while surrounded by people in the next cubicles working out the terms of the trade-in of their upside down car and working out a payment program for the next seven years for the next soon-to-be-upside down mistake.

A cocaine addict goes through hell to beat the habit. It is nearly impossible for a heroin addict to get and remain clean, and most never will. And a reformed alcoholic, will live the rest of their life just one step, one single action from falling back into that life, that life that was once a prison, the hell they worked so hard to escape from. But one thing they all have in common, they look at the still-afflicted with pity, and at themselves with great pride. Whether it was the lead cheerleader or the high school quarterback, the most popular, prettiest or most handsome, everyone has sometime looked at another with envy, and as we got older the object of envy may have gravitated toward position, status, or wealth. One thing is for sure, there's always been someone who it seems is doing better than you. As we continued into our adult lives, those same people, as well as almost everyone around us, seemed to have it all. In high school it was the best sneakers or most popular jeans, and now we're seeing everyone around us living in big houses, driving the nicest of cars, but this time, boy, we can be right there with them, in fact we could have a better car, a bigger house than the cheerleader or most popular person from back in school. It was all available to each of us, regardless of who we were, and suddenly, at least in our minds, we could compete with any of them. We're successful, we've got all the great stuff.

Guaranteed, when you get yourself debt free, start doing a better job at providing for your future, you'll likely be the person of envy when you retire early, living the life that most would long for while the cheerleader or quarterback that it seemed everyone envied may be wearing sneakers and jeans that aren't paid for, and will continue to be on the feeding tube until they die. Forget about everyone else, do this for yourself, or more importantly, for your spouse and family. After all, do you want to ultimately be a liability to your children? And speaking of your children, make the change today, admit your past mistakes to them and bring them along on this journey, help them to learn from your mistakes. Remember the alcoholic standing up at his first meeting? Plain and simple, no one is going to look after you except you, which is something we all have to realize. Wimpy was always pleading to "gladly pay Tuesday for a hamburger today." How do you suppose that made Wimpy feel? I want to say his name was very fitting.

Just like that first Hoody, the first bit of easy credit, well some may have been just a little suspicious, but then very soon it got easier and easier until it was a way of life. But like the baby squirrels, about half of the adult population of our country, including some of us and most of our children, it's all they've ever known, it most certainly has always been a way of life; it's where food comes from, it's where everything comes from. Just as bad health or eating habits early in life will greatly limit your quality of life in later years, same goes for the Hoody, even if you get off the habit, damage has been done, but hey, don't let that stop you from beating the habit, at least half a good life is undoubtedly better than no good life.

So, if you've been living your life for today, basically borrowing from and never worrying about your tomorrow, how many do you expect will be there to pay for your bad habits and selfishness when you very soon wake up older, broke, with worn out stuff and no means of support?

Well, the differential between the supported and supporters has been exponentially growing, so it's reasonable to expect that very soon, if we're not already almost there, the very few that have acted responsibly, possibly again just down to the one-percenters, will be the only ones left and able to care for all the rest. I'm thinking that neither will feel too good about it. Maybe we should ask Wimpy.

Anyone still reading at this point must have either found at least one point they could relate to and maybe even use to improve their own life, or you are reading on in disbelief that the author could actually manage to tick-off or demean just about anyone and everyone.

So, obviously, a majority of the American voters believed the hype and rhetoric of Barack Obama, most of which we've witnessed to be just that, and supported by empty, broken promises. As the American people were just beginning to suffer through a terrible self-induced hangover after going on a hellacious bender that lasted decades, of over spending and irresponsible actions, in pursuit of continued instant self-gratification, along came this guy who told us, "**It's not your fault.**" He told us all we were middle class, and that was being taken away. Why would any of us question it? After all, most of us had been living what appeared to be a globally-envied American middle class life, even though we didn't want to admit that we had borrowed it. **That's right; we borrowed our way up in class.** All the while, our government continued as it had for at least the past decade, promoting and enabling us. Why? Because, they are scared to death that when the spending stops, it will all collapse. So they keep the printing presses going, continue to run up massive debt themselves, handing out every imaginable tax credit and deduction in an effort to keep every penny in regular Americans' pockets, knowing that for every penny each citizen receives, they will spend three.

Then when the bloated American household debt reached a point where it had become totally unsustainable, and people bought everything and paid for very little, the bubble finally burst, leaving the government an obligation but at the same time an opportunity to choose between the responsible path, of letting the pain fall where deserved, on the masses of people who with greed and little thought had borrowed and spent far beyond their means, as well as the large financial firms that capitalized on people's greed and self-serving desires, or the bailout and forgiveness path. As we know, they chose the latter.

Our government leaders couldn't stand to take their medicine and suck it up. No, they chose to continue, in fact step up the massive accumulation of debt, in the trillions of dollars, to a point that bluntly put, is unfathomable, an act that should be considered treasonous. If they would have just let the marbles fall where they should have, and let the big banks that did bad things fail, let the people who should have never bought too big of house or too nice of car simply give them back, go broke, and start over, it would have been ugly, possibly uglier than what previously earned the designation "The Great Depression." But now, we would be back in business, with a growing robust economy and more importantly, we would have all learned a valuable lesson. As it is, the responsible people who bought a home, signed a promissory note (a promise to pay), and paid their payments as agreed upon, watched while the others, their friends, neighbors, and relatives stopped making their payments and were rewarded by being allowed to stay in their homes, payment and rent free, sometimes for years, then forgiven for their bad behavior and allowed to stay in their home, payments reduced to a lesser amount, and in many cases, large amounts of the debt were simply eliminated.

236

And as you would expect, just like a cancer, the same expectation and lack of personal responsibility spread to every personal obligation from student 'pizza and beer' loans to nearly endless unemployment benefits. It was "Poor me, it's not my fault," all the while some of the rest of us were left to pay our bills, only now we've taken on the burden of the Hoggy Hogs' obligations too. The government handpicked which big businesses and too-big-to-fail banks to bail out with more borrowed dollars, while each of their more responsible competitors looked on as some of us did, thinking, 'Hey, what about us?'

This went on at a time when we really needed our nation to be brought together, but instead it was being divided. By this time at least half of the nation's people were paying no income tax, basically bringing nothing to the party, yet they were constantly being told that they weren't getting their fair share. Maybe, just maybe someone should have questioned whether they are or ever have contributed their fair share.

I realize that it must be much easier to be Santa Claus, handing out gifts to the children, than to be the guy out front ringing the bell in the cold asking for donations. So what did we get? We got handouts, or handouts on steroids, when what was needed was a simple hand-up.

When I think of what I've witnessed since Barack Obama came onto the scene, I think of a 1960s movie with a bunch of school girls in frilly dresses all giggling and gossiping, grouped together as one in the middle is pointing her finger out at the girl who is left out, and putting her down, while the rest of the group nods and goes along. The more those girls listened to the instigator, the more she fed on it and continued the disgusting behavior. Then, as more girls joined the group, it just seemed more and more acceptable to put down and ridicule the less popular girl. I think each one of us have witnessed or even been part of a similar situation, either on one side or the other.

Mr. Obama found it to be quite a popular topic as a large chunk of the population were going through hard to handle times, adjusting to possibly having to go without much of what they had become very accustomed to getting, usually much before they could afford, to point at and ridicule the "haves," while gathering the rest, separating them and telling them that they are the "have-nots." He singled out the bankers, referring to them as "predatory lenders," all the while standing, gossiping to the "predatory borrowers," the ones that were failing to pay back as promised. He then went further, while standing in the group, gossiping and putting down people, he pointed out the CEOs of business, and soon the large group of his followers hated those guys, and from there the next to get picked on were people that had worked hard and paid their debts, worked hard and acted responsibly, anyone who had succeeded and excelled. He branded them as people who aren't paying their share. He did this at a time when the truth was just the opposite, in that they were the only ones paying taxes or contributing anything.

Instead of encouraging the American people to put forth the effort and reach for that brass ring, those opportunities still very much available in this country, he continued to put down the hard workers, the job creators, and the people who have been carrying the heavy burden. He continued to brainwash the group of followers into thinking that someone such as a CEO shouldn't be rewarded, that no one should make that much money, simply because it was more than they were making. He completely took the focus off of hard work and effort, taking risks and succeeding, and instead kept people focused on what they weren't getting. **He spoke of**

income inequality and wealth inequality with absolutely no mention of their direct correlation to effort inequality.

Very quickly, most anyone who had worked hard, saved some money, and acted responsibly was being pointed at, treated like the outsider, and being told that they didn't do it themselves, instead that the government had done it for them. One-percenter became a nasty term, when just so recently they had been able to hold their head high and show pride in what they accomplished. After all, this had always been considered the land of opportunity, and anyone who had worked hard and made it was considered to be a good example and continued the opportunities for others to do the same. Now, suddenly the emphasis was taken off hard work and personal responsibility, with people being instead encouraged and enabled to choose whether or not to even work.

The "Dirty Rotten Rich People," as they were made out to be, the very people who by this time were carrying the bulk of the burden, paying the large majority of the taxes, were told that they should pay more. **A large majority of the population was duped into believing the lies and deceit, and the voters blindly voted in anyone promising more free stuff, more sympathy for the irresponsible, which is entirely why, in such a short time, we went from enjoying a functioning government to what we see today: the most divisive group of people to ever lead our country.**

In both the Senate and House, we've got on one side those who realize that the present rate of spending and debt accumulation is so unsustainable that it will, without a doubt result in the total collapse and end of a once great nation. Some of these leaders just simply will not back down when confronted with the continuation of this idiotic mismanagement of a nation. And when they stand up for what they know to be right, they are ridiculed and treated like that girl on the outside. On the other side, we've got the ones that are too weak to make the tough decisions necessary to save our country, too afraid of losing their own positions to say no, and obviously too ignorant to know what's at stake, so they opt to just keep spending and printing money, spending and borrowing, spending and promising.

And if the massive borrowing to feed the gluttonous appetite of our domestic hand-outs weren't enough, these same elected leaders are continuing to bankrupt our nation by spending billions and supplying terrorist- harboring nations around the world with weaponry that will undoubtedly end up being used against us.

Plain and simple, here and abroad, we are feeding the wrong people.

As for the people of this nation, you and I, we had better come to the realization that everything is about to change and I'm talking very soon. Each one of us would be smart to get our own house in order because we cannot depend on the continued government feeding trough. In fact, more than not depend on it, you can almost count on it all running dry very soon. When the Hoody's run out, which will come much sooner than you think; it will be **EVERY SQUIRREL FOR HIMSELF**.

DON'T FEED THE SQUIRRELS

CPSIA information can be obtained at www.ICGtesting.com
Printed in the USA
BVOW09*1603101214

377683BV00002B/2/P

9 780990 906407